for the love of sister...

a Sibling's Story

For the Love of Sister...A Sibling's Story

"A moving saga of a family's journey back to wholeness fighting the enemy—cancer. A story of love, devotion strength, and spiritual enlightenment. Well written and moving."

Juanita Moffitt
American Legion Auxiliary President
Post 79, Yarnell, Arizona

"A *must* read! This story captures the true meaning of family and offers many life lessons if we open our hearts and minds to Nancy Seriani's words."

Jo Ann Speelman Dramer
Journalist/Reporter

for the love of sister...

a Sibling's Story

by Nancy Seriani

For The Love Of Sister…
Copyright © 2017 by Nancy Seriani.

Published in the United States of America
ISBN Paperback: 978-1-947765-22-1
ISBN eBook: 978-1-947765-23-8

All rights reserved. No part of this publication may be reproduced, stored in a retrieval system or transmitted in any way by any means, electronic, mechanical, photocopy, recording or otherwise without the prior permission of the author except as provided by USA copyright law.

The opinions expressed by the author are not necessarily those of ReadersMagnet, LLC.

ReadersMagnet, LLC
10620 Treena Street, Suite 230 | San Diego, California, 92131 USA
1.619.354.2576 | www.readersmagnet.com

Book design copyright © 2017 by ReadersMagnet, LLC. All rights reserved.
Cover design by Ericka Walker
Interior design by Shieldon Watson

This book is dedicated in honor of my sister's
life and to all the lives she touched.

Thanks to my husband for always loving me.

Acknowledgments

WITHOUT MY FAMILY THERE would be no story. It is only fitting then to credit them first and foremost.

Had it not been for some very special ladies: Helen, Nancy Marie, Robin, Barb, Juanita, and JoAnn, this story surely would not have been in your hands.

Thank you all so much. I am very grateful.

God Bless You,
Nancy Seriani

Contents

Foreword 11

The Unknown 13
The Plan 19
Forgiveness 25
Plan B 29
The Alternative 39
Retest 49
Rearrange Life Again 51
Get A Job 59
Retest and Rearrange 61
Siblings Stand United 65
Making Memories 69
Help From Beyond 77
Last Trip to the Hospital 83
The Last Ten Days 87
Hospice and Family 95
There is no Death, Only a Change of Worlds 107

Epilogue 119
Author Bio 121

Foreword

NANCY SERIANI IS A shining star. She always has a smile on her face. Nancy is the first one to walk up to a stranger in a crowd and make them feel welcome. I know, because that is just what she did for me. Nancy is my best friend. I love her like a sister.

God has touched Nancy with the ability to write her life experiences. *For the Love of Sister* will take you on a journey. Nancy and her family helped their sister, Nena, fight cancer. This book will make you smile, laugh, and cry. You will see the will in Nena to live. There will be battles won and, yes, battles lost. Cancer brings this family close together. You will be wishing that you had the close relationship between brothers and sisters as Nancy shares with her siblings.

I am so glad that the manuscript is no longer in a box on a closet shelf.

God bless you, Nancy Seriani.

Love ya,
Nancy Tschikof

The Unknown

It was in the fall of 1995. The colors of crimson, amber, gold, and orange blazed the hillsides of southwestern Wisconsin. Carrying into the garage armfuls of miscellaneous yard items, she fell. She picked herself up, brushed herself off, and continued putting away things in preparation of the upcoming winter months.

A few days later, she called her oldest sister, a bit concerned about the fall she had taken earlier in the week. "Nanc, what are you doing?" Nena asked.

"Oh, hi, baby girl. Just having coffee and visiting with George. How are you?"

"Okay," she replied, with some hesitation.

Recognizing that tone, as older sisters do, I said, "Something doesn't sound right about that 'okay'—what's the matter? Are Denny and the boys all right?" Nena assured me that her husband and sons were fine and began explaining about the fall she had taken.

"When I fell down, I landed on top of the wooden box I was carrying. I have a lump on my chest, Nanc, near my left breast."

"Is it like a bruise, baby, or what?"

"No, not a bruise-like a hard lump with a pea inside of it," she said.

"Would you feel better to have it looked at?" I instantly asked, sensing through the words she *didn't* say that she would feel better.

"Yes. Would you go with me? I'll make an appointment in Dubuque and call you back."

"Great. I'll be expecting your call."

Within an hour, she had called me back with an appointment for Friday. "I'll stop by and pick you up, Nanc. I have some errands to run in Dubuque after the doctor's appointment, and I'll buy lunch!"

"I'll be ready, sister, but please try not to worry about this—we'll wait and see what the doctor has to tell us."

"Okay, Nanc, I'll try. I love you, and I'll see you Friday."

The doctor assured us that, in his opinion, the lump was nothing to worry about and she should make another appointment in three months and he'd check it out again. She wasn't satisfied with this decision, and her concern continued to grow over the following week. There were no signs of bruising to attribute the lump to the fall. There was absolutely no reason my sister could come up with that this hard lump should be where it was.

She decided to call him back, schedule another appointment in one week, and have the lump examined again. Nena and Denny went together to the appointment.

I was working that day at The Outpost, a sporting goods store owned by our brother, Mark. When the phone rang, I answered and heard my baby sister's voice say, "Nanc, I've got breast cancer. They did a biopsy, and the results were positive." Through her tears and shaky voice, her fears were manifesting in her mind. She was frantic with the unknown.

"Nena, I'll be right there. By the time you and Denny get home, I'll be getting there too. I love you, sister, and I'll see you in a little bit."

Without thinking, I quietly explained to my brother about the news I just heard and apologized for leaving because the customers were backed up to the cooler doors. It was nearing the end of his busy season, and all of the Chicago visitors were in Wisconsin to enjoy the last of the beautiful weather, enjoying their vacation days until next year. I felt bad leaving him alone, but not bad enough to stay.

As I drove, I prayed out loud to be sure I would be heard, asking for strength and guidance and the right words to say to try to comfort my sister.

Only two and half years earlier, I had the same talk with my higher being after the doctors had diagnosed my husband, George, with lung cancer. One spot the size of a dime on one lung, a spot the size of a quarter on the other lung. The big *C* word. The word no one really understands until it enters the front door of their own home. Once it enters, it hangs in the air. Even when you know what it's like, it's still hard to know what to say to someone else.

The day they told us that George had cancer, George politely told his doctor, "Thank you for telling me what I've got," and walked out of the room. The doctor suggested a surgeon and perhaps chemo and radiation at the major University Hospital in Madison.

George wasn't going for any of the doctor's plans. He was already down the hall, headed out the door to the truck, when the doctor called my name. I turned back to acknowledge him. He told me that I had to change my husband's mind and attitude, that all of this would be made worse if he didn't get started with treatments right away.

I got within inches of his face. Quietly and sternly, I said, "Didn't you just hear my husband thank you for your professional opinion? He won't do any of your treatments. He'll live the best he can live until he doesn't live anymore. Meanwhile, can I count on you to write prescriptions for pain as he needs them?"

The doctor told me no, that he would not be part of anything like that and George should fine another doctor.

George, already fifty-five years old, had seen many people, family and friends, go through the whole cancer thing. To him, the end result had always been the same. Death. In his mind, the treatments he had seen given were far worse than cancer, itself. He had, most recently in his life, watched his father die of leukemia and a brain tumor. The doctors wanted to try this and that, do this and do that, until his mother said, "No more experimenting."

At that moment, George had made up his mind—if it ever happened to him, he would be a guinea pig for no one! For George, leaving the clinic that day without the appointments that had been recommended by the doctors was the absolute right thing to do.

For the next couple of months, George and I put all our affairs in order, including early retirement and disability from Social Security, getting the words just right on all the paperwork for the bureaucrats that had no idea what hell we were going through.

Endless pokes and probes by this doctor or that doctor. All the while sick. Going from a strong and healthy one hundred eighty pounds of hard-working man to a very weak, one hundred thirty pounds with a lot of pain. After he exhausted all the pain pills on the market, they started him on Morphine-pills, liquid, and patches. Without insurance to cover anything, we quickly went through the retirement pension that he'd worked thirty-eight years for.

Through it all, his attitude remained good. We helped our families address the issue of death in a positive fashion. We spoke of the cancer openly to everyone. George let them all see that death was not to be feared. He had lived his life to the fullest. He'd done it all…twice! He was grateful for his life. Whenever he was called, he would be ready to go. All the children in the family knew that "Uncle" would soon be an angel in heaven.

Two Thanksgiving and two Christmas holidays had passed by, and George started coming back. He started gaining weight, got color back in his face, and he began to feel better. He had rid the cancer from his body. Over the next few months, he improved greatly. Everyone was sure he was a walking miracle.

I had been given what I asked for on that first day. Would I be heard and helped again today as I once again begged for help?

When I arrived at Nena's, the door flew open, and Nena fell into my arms, sobbing, scared and trembling. "Oh, sister," I said, "be thankful you found the lump. Be thankful it presented itself to you."

"How can you say that? It's not fair! I have two boys to raise, and Denny needs me. I'm a good person, and I don't deserve this!" Nena cried. "I'm so mad! How could God do this to me?"

Trying to hold and comfort my sister with my touch, I replied, "I don't think it's God we should be mad at, baby girl. I think it's the cancer we should be mad at. The anger at the cancer will make you fight."

We held onto each other until I felt comfortable about leaving. I knew that the conversation Nena was going to have with Denny would be one that needed privacy. It wouldn't be easy to speak about, but decisions would have to be made, and the sooner the better.

I left for home to tell George of the news. I wasn't looking forward to this conversation, knowing in my heart that Nena would opt for any and all treatments available. I was sure that George would know that, too. On my way home, I begged that if there was any way to put Nena's cancer into my body to please do it. I knew it couldn't be and continued to pray for strength and courage and again the right words to say. I asked for the white light to surround sister, watch over her, and to keep Nena's family strong.

The night seemed endless. The thoughts were here, there, and all over-making no sense. Morning finally came, and the phone finally rang. It was Nena. "Nanc, I have another appointment tomorrow to decide what to do. Will you go with me?"

"Of course, dolly. What time is our appointment?" I asked.

"It's at 9:00 a.m. Denny and I will be by to pick you up."

"I'll be ready, babe. I love you. Bye."

The unknown made the night once again seem endless. Morning finally came, and, looking like the true picture of health,

Nena got out of the car and headed toward my front door. As she approached, so beautiful, so classy, so young, I wondered how long I would be able to hold her and touch her?

To me, Nena was without a doubt the most beautiful girl ever born. She maintained her hourglass figure after the birth of her sons, Chase and Cole Jesse. She had eyes of blue, perfect brown hair, and a face like no other. She was stylish, always totally matched, gold jewelry…the works. She had a look that was all Nena. Wherever she went, she would turn heads. I could see in my little sister's beautiful, passionate blue eyes the anger, fear, and doubts of the unknown. We hugged and kissed and, after telling George to have a good day, we headed into a world that would change our lives forever.

The Plan

HEADING DOWN THE ROAD, Denny and I made small talk about any and every thing not having to do with cancer. The fifty-mile ride seemed to take days. Once there, we found where we had to be and waited for the nurse to call Nena's name. It was an oncology waiting room with a few plastic plants, some magazines, and a coffee machine.

Waiting for their names to be called, people sat in wheelchairs with numerous bags hanging on poles over their heads, some without any hair, and some with a bucket sitting on their lap. And no one was speaking. It seemed to me that all the people, who were obviously patients, had no family member or friend with them.

I decided to ask Nena if she wanted a cup of coffee. She did, and so started the small party in the waiting room. I asked everyone if they'd like a cup of coffee and how they took it or if they just wanted a cup of fresh water. Conversations started up by telling each other where they were from, what the experts were saying the winter would be like, and what a wonderful hospital we were in.

Soon, the nurse was calling for Nena. We were escorted to the same doctor's office we had been in for the first visit, when we were told that the lump was nothing to worry about. The doctor introduced himself to Denny and began laying out the options for Nena. He had no bedside manner and was very matter-of-fact about the whole thing, but Nena clung to his every word. She could have the entire breast removed or just the lump. Whichever she decided to do, the procedure would be followed up by chemotherapy and radiation treatments. The only other possible drug involved would be an anti-nausea medication to help with the treatments.

I asked about alternative treatments, including vitamins, herbs, or tonics that would possibly enhance her recovery. He was somewhat reluctant about my questions but was passive, saying there was no medical or scientific proof that such things were helpful, but that he didn't care if she took them.

Over the last several years, while my husband George lay dying, I researched and studied the healing effects of certain natural remedies. I slowly started introducing these natural treatments into George's daily ritual. I thought that because of the constant, violent, daily upheaval of poisons out of his body, there was a great need to replenish his immune system. He was not able to keep food down long enough for it to be helpful for healing, so if he could get any healing inside from other sources, it would aid in his recovery. All the hours of concentrating and calculating I had spent reading books had paid off. George was stronger and healthier. I was sure, in my mind, that prayer and natural alternatives had saved George.

Now, hearing this doctor talk to my sister about this subject with his somewhat judgmental and negative attitude, I swallowed hard, bit my tongue, and continued taking notes while the doctor gave his speech. Denny asked if we could speak to the doctor that would be giving the chemotherapy and radiation treatments before any decisions were made, and we were taken to another office where we met with the other doctor.

He examined Nena and her history file. It became immediately clear to us that this doctor was of a loving, carrying nature. He explained what he knew about breast cancer and the treatments offered in a way that ordinary people could understand.

While looking over her history, the doctor directed his questions toward me, asking if I was the sister who, many years earlier, had had both breasts removed because of fibrocystic disease. I answered, "Yes."

"Explain to me, please," asked the doctor, "how this determination was made."

"I suffered with pain most all of my adult life," I began, "until I was at the point where I would have to hold myself while riding in a car." I crossed my arms over my chest in a hugging gesture to show the doctor what I meant. "When I took a shower, I stood with my back to the showerhead because I couldn't stand to have the water hit me."

I explained that I had decided to see the specialists at an institute in Phoenix, Arizona, where I lived at the time. For the next seven years, I followed a regimen of exercise, vitamins, and herbs, with no caffeine or dairy products. The improvement was only slight and didn't last very long. They explained to me that we all have cancer cells in our bodies, and, if and when these break loose and try to find a place to multiply and grow, they will seek areas of the body that are already compromised for whatever reason.

"Chances were that if that happened to me, the cells would go directly to my breasts. They talked about preventative medicine, whereby eliminating the situation before the problem presented itself. This was advanced research in those days. It made perfect sense to me, and it was one of the best decisions I felt I ever made for myself."

He looked at Nena and said, "That is one of the smartest women I've ever met. In the years to come, we'll be seeing more of this radical preventative medicine taking over, and the end result will be women living longer."

Nena's mind was spinning with questions, but she felt comfortable enough to ask the doctor, "If I was your wife, what would you tell me to do?" He quietly said, "I would tell my wife to have both breasts removed."

We all thanked him for his time and went outside the hospital and found a place to sit, so we could talk about all the things we had been told. The conversations between us was calm as we kept going over and reviewing the notes I had taken.

Nena's decision was becoming clear. She concluded that the right thing, for her, was to have surgery and have the lump removed. She would do the treatments prescribed after surgery, and the cancer, she knew, would then be gone. With that, we made the necessary appointments for surgery and left the hospital for the journey home.

Trying to lighten the heavy tension in the car, I assured sister she should be proud of her decision. "You feel in your heart that this is what you should do, then that's what is right for you, baby. Only you can make that decision. Not me. Not Denny. No one but you. Now you've got a plan, and you know what you've got to do. I'll be with you every step of the way. So will Denny. You're not going to do this alone, my baby girl. I'm going to be there. We'll hang out and do the treatments; we'll do lunch, and we'll shop and spend all of Denny's money!"

Through her tears, Nena managed to laugh, and, before long, we were laughing, talking, and making plans around cancer.

The surgery was a success. The surgeon was confident that the margins were clear (just a fancy term that means they thing they "got it all"). Soon after, the chemotherapy treatments started.

It was a dreary room, long and narrow, with several reclining dentist-looking chairs. Patients filled all the chairs with bags and bags of liquid medicine hanging overhead, dripping into their veins. The room had windows about waist-high lining one long wall that looked out at concrete buildings. The sky above and beyond those buildings told of an upcoming winter storm. The hospital inside looked like what I felt: cold, unrelenting, and uncertain. At the end of the row of chairs in the corner was an empty chair that was waiting for Nena. Next to it was a straight-back chair that I claimed for myself.

We greeted all our fellow patients as we made our way to the chairs. I set up house in that little corner, making sure that everything was just right and that baby sister would be comfy. I spotted the pillows and blankets on the way in and made Nena snug as a bug while the magic medicine ran through her.

We laughed and talked and made plans for the upcoming holidays. Each treatment day, we looked forward to being together. We'd have cappuccino on the way to get the treatment and talk about each other's previous night. During the treatments, we paid our bills, made out our Christmas cards, and even got caught up on organizing our tax papers for filing in January. Some days, Nena would sleep through the treatments. But for the most part, she was on top of her game, never letting anyone see her out of control about cancer.

After the treatment, we'd do lunch or maybe shop or run errands. The car trips, there and back, were never quiet. We talked about family, friends, and life. We completely stayed away from talking about death. Nena was sure that if she even had a thought about it, that it would jinx her. She made that clear with me, Denny, and the doctors from the get-go.

Nena tolerated the treatments well. Other than one short hospital stay for an infection at the surgical site, and her radiated breast, hard as stone and terribly discolored, she was doing remarkably well. They assured her that this was normal. The doctors were confident that the surgery and treatment had worked; they would retest in three months.

Overwhelmed with joy and hope, Nena felt she had beaten the cancer. She won. Life for Nena was good again, and she got back into her more normal routine. She had managed to keep her home running as normal as possible since her diagnosis, but now, instead of running for treatments, she would be home.

Cancer was not going to get her down. Besides, she had beaten it!

Forgiveness

It was Christmas, and there were many things to get done: shopping, wrapping gifts, cleaning, decorating, and baking. She did them all. She did more.

Christmas dinner was to be at Mark's house. George and I arrived early to help Mark and his wife, Barbara, get everything ready. Shortly after Denny, Nena, and the boys arrived, our other sister Amy; her husband, David; and their three children arrived. Scottie, our other brother; his wife, Cathy; and their four children followed. All the cousins were happy to be playing together, as were the siblings and their spouses.

We had all gathered for an afternoon of fun, food, gifts, and games. With everyone's busy schedules, some of the family hadn't seen Nena, so they were quietly saddened and surprised at how she looked. She was wearing a short, straight brown wig since treatments had made her hair fall out and her coloring was not good. She acted as though nothing was wrong with her. She had a healthy appetite, as usual, and just enjoyed being with the family.

I had been the messenger for Nena with the other siblings so everyone would know, at all times, what was going on with her progress. There had been some tension over the years that caused some problems between some of the siblings, so with me being the communicator, I took advantage of the role I was in.

I had spoken to each one, trying to make them understand the complexity of this disease.

In order for Nena to heal and for all of them to heal, they must let things go, give it up, and go on. Go on in a way that benefits everyone. Forgiveness. I had many talks with each one. Slowly, they all began to want to start somewhere to help in this healing process. It would be for the betterment of the family.

It was Mark who made the invitation for Christmas dinner to all the siblings, their spouses, and their children. The day was filled with good times and good food, exactly what I prayed for. I was so proud of all my siblings for their open minds and willingness to want to make a change. It was not something that came natural to any of them. They would all have to work at it and become self-taught, but I knew they all would do it successfully.

Winter was in full swing. Weeks went by, and before long it was time to be retested. We made plans to go together.

Nena was sure that all the results would be positive. I agreed with her no matter what she said, keeping my own thoughts about everything to myself. The views Nena had were exactly the opposite of mine.

I quietly questioned everything about cancer and the treatments. Everything one sister adamantly believed in, the other sister adamantly believed something altogether different. I never let my thoughts and feelings be known to my baby sister.

The appointment day for retesting was a sunny day, but it was bitterly cold outside. Inside the car, as two sisters drove to Dubuque, the conversation was warm, happy, and upbeat. Nena and I talked about the past Christmas holiday and how much it had meant to Nena to be with the family. She and her own family had been excluded for so many years. This had triggered the feelings again for her family connection.

Nena had an estranged relationship with some of her siblings after she married Denny. It had hurt her deep inside but was proving to all of them that they had been wrong. Her husband

a Sibling's Story

was a good man, a good provider, and they had two wonderful little boys together. It's really all she ever wanted. But there was always her longing to belong to the sibling connection.

Nena thanked and praised me for the role I played in the reuniting of all the siblings, spouses, and children. It was a burden that needed lifting, and, whatever it was that brought about the change, Nena was forever grateful.

Nena did all the tests that day and was told that the results would be back in a couple of days. They would call and let her know. We left, had our lunch at a restaurant, and headed home, talking about the upcoming spring and gardens and flowers. It was the weekend, so we knew we'd hear nothing until Monday at the soonest. Nena promised that she'd call as soon as she heard anything.

It was Monday, 2:00 p.m., when the phone rang. I answered and heard Nena crying on the other end. The cancer was back. The chemo and radiation had not stopped it. Nena was hysterical. I said, "I'll be right there."

When I arrived, Nena was alone. Denny was still at work, and the boys were still at school. We held each other and cried at the table.

"Thank God they found this out. Be glad they told you this now so you can get another plan and give it hell again. If they found this out later, it may have been too late. You've got to get a plan, sister, and you have to make it happen. You need to talk this over with Denny and see what he says. Make another appointment to hear what they have to say and what your options are."

Nena stopped crying and began to pull herself together. She needed to get supper started. She also needed to tell Denny. And how would she ever be able to tell the boys?

She busied herself in the kitchen while I folded some laundry for her. Nena talked aimlessly while I just listened. We both calmed ourselves as we worked. I left Nena to spend a little time alone before her family came home. She promised to call if she needed anything.

Plan B

THE FOLLOWING MORNING, NENA called to tell me she scheduled a conference with the doctor and to ask if I would go along with her. It was for the next day.

On the ride to the doctor's office, I wrote down questions that we wanted answers to. Nena was scared, but mostly she was mad. Mad at the doctor who said he had gotten it all. Mad at the chemo and radiation. Mad at the whole damn cancer thing. She was loaded with questions and demanded answers in the conference. The questions she didn't ask, I asked.

The doctor had very little to say, other than that she had a very aggressive cancer and perhaps since they weren't able to help her that she should go someplace else. She agreed, and he suggested the cancer specialists in Iowa City. His nurse did all the calling, and she scheduled all the necessary appointments.

We drove home, after a totally exhausting day hearing everything we didn't want to hear. I called George from the car phone and asked him to meet me at Nena's. We all ate supper together, put the boys to bed, and the four of us went into the den. Nena and I began explaining to our husbands all that we had been told. There was a blizzard outside that night and somewhat of a blizzard inside, as well. The four of us discussed all angles of what to do.

Sometime during the night, it was decided to call the family doctor in Madison to ask if she could see him. Dr. Mack answered the phone at his home, and Nena explained as best she could about everything that had gone on since October of the previous year. He told her that he could help her and to call his office and make an appointment for consultation, and to be sure to bring all her medical records, X-rays, and test results. This doctor was so kind. He made Nena feel so much better with just his words. He had been Denny's family doctor for many years. He was a specialist, a surgeon, and was highly trusted by Denny's family. We could now all rest for the night.

After the snowplow had gone by, the kids got on the bus, Denny left for work, George left for home, and we headed for Dubuque.

The driving was slow, with all the snow and slush on the roadways, but we were on a mission. About halfway there, Nena placed a call to Madison from the car phone. Julia, Dr. Mack's nurse, had been expecting her call and had already scheduled Nena for tests and a consultation for the following morning. Julia explained that it would be a full day, but that Dr. Mack was eager to begin. She reassured Nena that everything would be all right and she must be a very special person to have the doctor take such a personal interest in her healthcare.

After the conversation, we talked about how good everything was turning out. One doctor seemed like he couldn't wait to see her transferred someplace else while another doctor was welcoming her, at least offering her hope.

As we went from floor to floor, office to office, gathering records, charts, and films, we had feelings of rejection, failure, and animosity toward the hospital, doctors, and staff. I was very happy to be rid of them all. I never did like the atmosphere of the hospital or the uncaring feelings of the majority of the staff. I felt they treated my sister as if she were just a number.

As we sat eating our lunch at the hospital cafeteria, several nurses, radiation technicians, and chemo nurses passed by us without a word. We eventually left, took all we had come for, and left Dubuque without every looking back.

Denny, Nena, and I were back on the road at four thirty the next morning, ready for another day, hoping we would hear some answers that we wanted to hear.

The mood seemed different at this hospital. Everyone seemed so friendly.

As Nena was testing, Denny and I talked in the waiting room. In between tests, the three of us would be together, waiting for the next test or X-ray. The day was a long one. Nena was exhausted from all the poking and prodding.

The results of all the tests were in. The three of us and Dr. Mack got together to discuss the findings. Yes, it was true: the cancer was back in the same breast. Even after the chemo and radiation, he feared it may also have gone into the lymph nodes. All her counts were good; age was on her side, and she had healed from everything prior. He felt it would be in her best interest to have the breast removed and also take a pocket of lymph nodes out to put through pathology.

Once the surgery was over, she would again need some chemo or radiation or both. That decision would be made at that time by another doctor. He felt that her young age of thirty-six was on her side, for healing, but that this particular kind of cancer was very aggressive in younger women like her. He was hopeful that he could help her.

The meeting was good and helpful. Nena felt like she'd made the right decision by seeing this doctor. She told him she'd make the decision and call back.

The trip home was quiet. All three of us were exhausted, and all three minds were spinning in circles. Nobody really knew what to say. We all knew that Nena was the one who would have to make the decision.

They dropped me off at my house, where George waited nervously to hear what had happened. He waved to them as they pulled out of the driveway and opened the door, grabbing me and holding me. He had missed me all day and knew that a lot had happened since I left our house that morning.

We stayed up half the night talking things over. I conveyed to George that I wished Nena would have both breasts removed but, whatever sister decided, I'd go right along with it, whether I believed in it or not. I'd wait until Nena called me instead of me calling her. I couldn't even imagine what was going through my sister's head. Denny…the boys…cancer…treatments…decisions. I wondered all night. I prayed all night.

The phone at Nena's house was constantly ringing. People concerned, hospitals scheduling appointments, labs giving results of blood tests, insurance people always asking the wrong questions at the wrong time. She was bombarded with calls, so I was the one who called our siblings to let them know what was going on. They always appreciated the calls, even though I began to feel like the messenger of doom and gloom. We all felt free to say whatever we wanted to each other during these calls, and, of course, each had something to say.

There had always been tension between Amy and Nena, since they were little girls. Although Nena had all the looks and beauty, Amy had the brains and the athletic abilities. Later on in life, Nena graduated from a trade school while Amy graduated from a major university. Nena could dress a window, and Amy could draw your blood, do the lab work, and hand you the calculated report she worked up.

When Amy married David, Nena was her maid of honor. Although Nena was happy about this, she was a little jealous. David's family had been on that farm for many years. It was customary with dads and their sons that, when the son was ready to marry, he would take over the family farm and the folks would move, usually to town or to the new house they built. Amy was able to move into a beautiful farmhouse with five hundred acres of land, a yard handsomely landscaped and had money in the bank, not to mention the great job she had doing blood work at a clinic very close to home.

At that time, Nena was working in the sales department in a furniture store. She was dating Denny, and, more times than not, their relationship was rocky and unreliable. One week she'd be happy and the next week not. They'd live together for a while, and then they wouldn't. During some of the rough times, Nena would call on her family to help get her out of situations. We always helped and got her straightened out, but before long Nena would go back with Denny. There was a general dislike for Nena always going back to Denny, so the tension only escalated over the years. Everyone was affected by it.

We came from a rather dysfunctional home, as kids anyway, and nobody wanted to see their baby sister get into another one as an adult. When times weren't good between Nena and Denny, she would defend him to her family. She just wanted to be loved, get married, and raise a family. She loved Denny no matter what. There had been physical confrontations between Denny and the family, confrontations that some family members couldn't let go of. In spite of it all, Nena loved Denny, and they were married.

Not many family members from our side were at their wedding. George and I were, even though I, too, had very mixed emotions. She was the perfect picture of a bride as our grandfather escorted her down the path that led to the arch where Denny handsomely waited for her. It was a beautiful day in mid-August. They looked so happy as they exchanged their vows.

Nena was determined to make her marriage work, not only for herself, but to show some others they were wrong and she was right.

Nena and Denny worked hard, played hard, and fought hard. In spite of everything, Nena was happy but desperately wanted a baby. She had known from the beginning with Denny that he didn't want to have more children. He had two from his previous marriage that they took care of together a lot of the time. Nena enjoyed the kids very much, even though there were constant battles between Denny and his ex-wife. But Nena wanted something more. All she ever wanted, since she was a little girl, was to have a husband who loved her and her own family.

Nena eventually did get pregnant, and the stipulation was made that "you wanted him, you raise him." After a strenuous labor and delivery, she bore her son, Chase. Three years later, she delivered Cole Jesse into the world. My sister was so happy. She had everything she ever wanted—a husband, stepchildren, and her two boys.

They sold their house in town and bought a farm, just as they had planned.

Denny worked outside the home at a nearby battery factory, and she was a stay-at-home mom. They had lots of animals. She raised baby calves and wiener dogs, and there was always a miscellaneous multitude of barnyard critters everywhere you looked. The garden was so big you'd have thought she was raising an army. The house was always undergoing some kind of major home improvement. She was a busy girl but loved it.

Nena and Denny were usually the ones to host the family get-togethers. It was mostly always for his side of the family, but George and I were always invited and always attended. They could definitely put on the feed.

Nena was a great cook and even a better baker. She was the queen of the kitchen when it came to cooking any wild game. She and Denny were avid hungers, and the freezers were always full. She did it all—tromped through the woods (usually in the cold winter months), tracked the animal, shot it, gutted it, skinned it, and butchered it. Their main red meat was venison, so she mastered the art of cooking with it.

I had felt, over the years, a special kind of friendship with Denny's family. They always felt bad for Nena and the relationship she had with her family. They always made Nena feel like she was their own, and I had always been grateful to them for that.

While speaking to each sibling on the phone, I said I'd call as soon as Nena decided what to do and when. I called Nena the following morning. Denny had already gone to work, the boys were off to school, and she was crying.

Soon the crying stopped and the anger took over. She was so mad at everything. She was mad at the world. Cancer does that! It turns your world upside-down. You have to learn to schedule your life around cancer. No matter how well you try to handle it, it ends up handling you!

Questions and answers you would never have believed, you have to deal with. Decisions have to be made that normally occur much later in life. She ranted on until she was satisfied she'd gotten it all out. I tried to help her see the positive side of it all. I tried to cover everyone's attitudes and opinions by always coming up with some excuse.

When she started talking about suing the previous doctors and hospital, even though I agreed with her, it was ultimately her decision to let them do what they did. I continued, over the years that followed, to try to discourage this. I wanted her to have as little stress in her life as possible. I watched, over the weeks and months to come, as she spent endless, countless hours with calls and letters, to no avail.

She finally said that she'd decided to have both breasts removed and do the treatments that should surely cure it. She said she'd call back with the schedule for surgery, and she did. It was scheduled in one week.

During the days prior to surgery, the schedule included many tests and drawing lots of blood. The hospital staff was very nice to us, but I always thought there was such a cold feeling in the place. After all, it was a university hospital.

I had, at one time in my life, worked at one of these hospitals in another state. People are better off not knowing what goes on in these places. I never said anything to my sister. She loved her doctor, the staff, and the hope they gave her. If Nena was happy, I was happy.

We were usually starved after testing, so we always got to eat out. She always treated me for going along with her. I was always glad to go with her, as it was obvious to everyone, by now, that our parents weren't going to be involved in this. I also felt a responsibility to my sister. I liked watching over her, trying to keep her calm, and loving her. I tried to help her find the rights in all the wrongs. Sometimes I could and sometimes I couldn't. One thing was for sure—I was intending to be there for her because it's what I wanted to do.

We got through all the tests, and it was the day of the surgery. She'd decided, to be on the safe side, to have both breasts removed. During the surgery, the doctors took lymph nodes from under the arm as well, and they were sent to pathology.

After sister had been in her room for a while, the doctors came back with the results. Yes, there were still cancer cells in the breast that had previously undergone treatment, and the majority of nodes, from under the opposite arm, were positive, as well.

Nena was devastated. Of course, she wanted to know what they could do for her. This doctor was only a surgeon, and he was now out of the picture, so they sent in the oncology doctor.

The female oncologist began by reiterating what the surgeon said, only she went into more detail. She explained about this very aggressive cancer and that since Nena was so young it would grow very quickly, as we were already seeing. She told Nena what her plan would be for treatment-chemo and radiation. But there were no guarantees.

Nena was very upset and angry. The doctor lacked bedside manner, and my sister felt that this doctor was offering no hope. She told the doctor to leave the room, in no uncertain terms.

The night was very long. She cried and sobbed and tried so desperately to make sense of it all. She was determined, by morning, that she did not want to see that particular oncologist ever again and made it known to the staff.

I wanted for Denny to come to the hospital to be with her. They could talk and try to make decisions. I left and went home.

The Alternative

ALL THE WAY HOME, I kept thinking that perhaps now might be just the right time to introduce her to an alternative. I had been implementing different herbs and vitamins into her daily routine of prescriptions drugs since her diagnosis, but it wasn't enough. I knew about a place that was doing wonderful things with cancer patients using alternative medicine. I didn't know a lot about it, but I knew someone who did.

When I got home, I told George to get ready because we were going for a ride. We drove to Dubuque and went to a health food place I knew. When I was there shopping, while George was sick, I became acquainted with a very knowledgeable woman. This kindly woman shared her thoughts and recommendations with me about his health and healing.

Every few months, I was back to replenish his supply. I saw positive results with George. After Nena was diagnosed, I started buying her a few things there. At first, Nena was reluctant to start taking the vitamins because her first doctor had been so negative about any supplements doing any good. She had his words stuck in her head, but she was also very aware that something had helped bring George back from the depths of despair. She knew part of it had to do with the vitamins and minerals he started taking.

The lady was there when we arrived, and I immediately asked about the small hospital we had spoken of in our earlier conversation. She knew just what I was referring to and got up to get a book. It was called *Beating Cancer with Nutrition*.

This lady actually had customers who had gone there, and they were doing very well. I took down all the information and the 800 number so Nena could call and talk to them. After everything the woman told me and everything I quickly read through, I was convinced that sister should at least call and explain her condition to see what they could offer. I looked at the map and determined it would be a four-to five-hour drive to get there. It was across the state of Wisconsin, into Illinois.

I thanked the woman, and then George and I left. I was excited to have this information, but I was also very nervous to bring it up to Nena. I prayed all night, asking God to give me the strength I needed to present this to my sister.

The following morning, I went back to Madison to be with Nena. I figured if a sign presented itself, then I would know the timing was right.

She told me everything she and Denny talked about the previous day and that she had cried most of the night. She said the surgeon told her that she did not need to use the oncologist and he'd suggest a different one for her. She just didn't know what to do or how to think. She knew cancer was bad, the treatments were worse and the side effects were even worse than all of it. "There just has to be some other way, Nanc," Nena said through her tears and shaky voice. That was my sign.

I began to explain to her what I had done after I left the hospital the day before. I explained everything I read and everything I had heard. I handed her the paper with the phone number on it. She reached over for the phone and dialed the number. The answering party said "Cancer Treatment Center of America. How can I help you?"

On the other end of that phone, my sister found the answer she'd been looking for: so much kindness and compassion and understanding that she was listening to. The gentle man she was speaking to suggested before she committed herself to the hospital's plan of treatment that maybe she could bring her records, be examined, and have a consultation by the staff at the treatment center in Zion, Illinois. He explained that the center would cover the costs she incurred for traveling expenses; even if she chose to fly, they would also arrange that.

I was sensing a calm cover over Nena as she lay on the stark white sheets of this hideously stark white room, talking to a voice that was giving her some hope. She gave the gentle voice at the other end no final answer. She needed time to think and time to talk to Denny. She'd call him back.

She was excited, and I was very happy that she was. She spoke to Denny, but there were so many unanswered questions. Little did we know that the gentle voice that she spoke to on the phone had overnight-expressed an information and material package to her. We all had a look at it. Denny and Nena seemed reluctant and skeptical.

These treatment plans were unheard of in the field of modern medicine. Fractioned doses of chemo, low dose radiation, herbs, vitamins, supplements, visualizations, imagery techniques, and the process of learning about the power that waits within. I was up for all of this; the others were not too excited. Some even thought it sounded more like a place where old hippies sat around and smoked dope all day. Oh! The conditioned minds of the general public.

Ultimately, Nena decided that she wanted to go to Zion to see what they had to say and what they could offer her. It would take a few days, so Denny would have to stay with the boys and go to work while she and I would drive to Zion, Illinois. It was decided. She called Zion, made the arrangements, and we left with all the records, charts, and test results in hand for a world that would change everything, or so we had hoped.

Physically, Nena was doing great after the mastectomy. Mentally and emotionally, she was doing better with this new hope she had been given. The drive was great. We stopped about halfway to eat supper, and about six hours after we'd left my house, we were in Zion, Illinois.

They put us up in a room across the street from the hospital. The next morning, we were up and ready to go meet a new world. We walked into the hospital through the small rotating front door into the lobby. We just stood there, looking around and at each other in total amazement. It was so beautifully decorated. A chandelier hung from the ceiling. There was dark antique furniture, wallpaper, carpet, and fresh bouquets of flowers. The feeling of it all was very calming and gratifying.

Polly was the volunteer at the desk. All hospitals should have a Polly at their front desk. We felt like we were definitely in the right place. Polly made us feel right at home. She was overwhelmed at my sister's beauty. She gave each of us a card to wear and then showed us the way to the cafeteria. The hospital was small, and that made getting around so much easier than the big university hospitals. Everyone was friendly and helpful.

"First," she said, "you'll have your breakfast." The cafeteria was also beautiful. Not only were the furnishings beautiful, but the food was healthy, natural, and displayed just right. Behind the hot food counter, a young woman took our order. The entire staff was friendly and outgoing. We got to the register to pay and were told that patients and their guests eat for free.

Our first stop after our gourmet breakfast was a fairly good-sized room where patients and their families waited to speak to a doctor about the different ways to deal with cancer. It was decorated like the lobby: wallpapered walls with dark colored wainscoting, thick piled carpet, and rich luxurious overstuffed couches and very comfortable matching recliners with end tables, coffee tables, and lamps for reading. Fresh baked muffins, fresh fruit, juice, coffee, and hot tea were also available. This was not your normal waiting room!

All the people in there were just like us—new to this hospital and overwhelmed by the ways of this hospital, all anxiously looking forward to speaking to a new staff of doctors. People were from all over the country. They all heard about this place from one source or another, but everyone's goal, in this room, was the same. They were all amazed at Nena's beauty and found it hard to believe that she had cancer. Each of them were there seeking alternative solutions.

A young woman approached us, beautifully dressed, and extended her hand to Nena. She introduced herself as the nurse of the doctor that Nena would be seeing. She sat with us and explained, quietly and calmly, the plan for the day. Then she walked us down the hall to the consultation room. Even the hallways were handsomely decorated.

The nurse sat us at a round table, and when the doctor arrived, she made all the proper introductions. He and the staff had read all of Nena's records, studied her scans, and reviewed all that we had brought. I took notes as he spoke. Nena asked questions, and he answered. At no time did we feel hurried or pushed or that this doctor needed to be someplace else. He was a surgeon, and he requested that Nena speak with all of the staff, as they would all be involved in any treatments. After she spoke to each of them, they would consult and then tell her what they thought to be the best plan for her.

Each doctor and each nurse was better than the ones before. I felt like this was the very first time that Nena was really hearing the truth. And she believed it because these people had gained her trust and confidence. They were teaching her a different way, and she liked what she was hearing.

We each rested peacefully that night in the hotel room. Nena called home and told Denny everything she could remember, and then I told him the rest. We would be returning home the following evening with the rest of the information.

The team of doctors had given her a lot to think about. They offered her options. Nena had spoken with many of the other patients and asked questions of them and their families. We felt at ease. It was obvious to me that after two days in Zion, my sister was ready to commit herself and her disease to the alternative treatments offered to her.

On the way back home, we discussed how she'd handle this with Denny. There would have to be sacrifices made on everyone's part. I told her that she needed to make a decision that she would be comfortable with and that everything after that would fall right into place. I knew she'd feel a lot better about everything after she talked to Denny and got his approval.

George was anxiously awaiting my return. Nena and I both were in good spirits, and he was happy to see us. She was excited to tell him all about what we'd experienced in Zion.

I asked her to call me later, and she said that she would. She was then out the door, anxious to get back to her family. She always hated leaving her boys and was longing to hold them again.

Several hours had passed when the phone rang. While we were in Zion, Denny had been talking to his family and different friends. They were all concerned about Nena leaving the mainstream of things. Nena was familiar with Madison, the staff of doctors; it was closer to home, and it was a university hospital with all the newest of modern technology. He didn't agree with this change and walked out of the house. That's when she called and asked if I would come over with the notes and talk to Denny with her.

George and I left right away. You could feel the tension in the air as we walked in the front door. Denny was surprised to see us, so I told him we'd come to show him the notes I'd taken. I was sure Nena couldn't remember everything. He was grateful, and we sat down to discuss all the findings. He became interested and curious but was still very unsure. I suggested that he go there and see for himself, ask the questions he needed answers for, and then see how he felt about things. Denny consented.

It was decided that the four of us would go to Zion and take their motor home as well as drive her car. If Nena decided to stay, many of the treatments would be done on an outpatient basis; we'd save money for the hotel expenses, and the guys would have the car to drive back home.

It didn't take Denny long to start feeling the same way Nena felt about Zion. Every question he raised was answered in a positive and professional manner with a twist of understanding and compassion. Their answers were simple: treat the body, the mind, and the spirit.

During one of the sessions, I saw a tear stream down Denny's face as the doctor spoke of the strength and determination of these patients. I believe he knew, just then, that this was the best place that his wife could be.

Later that day, Nena gave the go-ahead to the staff that she was ready to begin treatment. Denny and George left early that evening, knowing this was the right decision that Nena made.

Nena was determined to beat this cancer, and she felt that these people were going to help her do just that. It was great to see sister so positive and hopeful.

It was at this hospital that we started to get a real education about cancer and its victims. I found that they treated family members as well as they treated the patients. Families were just as important in the healing process as any of he treatments were. Everyone soon knew us as "the sisters."

During the next few months, Nena had the treatments and followed the regimen to the best of her ability. We'd stay three or four days at a time and then travel back home. We looked forward to the trips since during this time we felt free to talk or cry or scream. She tolerated all the treatments very well. The results of any of the tests she had done (and there were many) were back within hours. All things were looking good. The worse part of it all, for Nena, was leaving the boys.

During one of our trips, we brought Cole Jesse with us. The staff welcomed him with open arms. He managed to steal the show all four days we were there. He was absolutely the five-year-old wonder boy with all the right manners. Nena was so proud.

The time had come to see if the treatments had been successful. *Yes!* She got a clean bill of health. She would be retested again in a few months, but from the looks of things, she was good to go.

From that point on, she went right back into the normal mode. She could once again have a life that didn't have to be planned around a doctor's appointment or a treatment. She went on about her daily, normal routine, as usual. She pushed herself, always taking on more than two women should. She did the inside work, the outside work and took care of the boys, the husband, the families, the friends, the schools, the bus drivers, and the bill collectors. And deep down there, somewhere, lurked that nagging little thing called cancer.

Three months later, she was retested from top to bottom, and again, everything looked really good. She should continue doing whatever she was doing. The tests were good and the counts were good. She was told to come back in three months.

Nena was very grateful to the staff at Zion. She brought home-baked Amish friendship bread for them all, knowing that she would be getting good news. They were overwhelmed at her appreciation and even more so that she herself had baked it. The bread later became known as "Some'a Nena Bread." It was a name the family gave the recipe because only Nena made it for us.

She could hardly wait to get home and let Denny and the boys know the good news. She figured life was finally back to normal. She was elated at the thought that the cancer was surely gone for good after two great checkups in this six-month period.

She mentioned a vacation to Tennessee, to visit some friends and maybe going even farther, to the D.C. area, so they could check out some history of the country. She had it all planned out. And so it was the Nena's life became very normal again. She was immediately into her old routine.

There was a giant garden to plant, as well as flowers, a yard to mow, weeds to pull, cattle to feed and keep watered, hay to bale, shopping, cooking, canning, cleaning, laundry, swimming classes, birthday parties, and on and on the list goes. I used to wonder if I was lazy because I couldn't get half of this done! That little girl could wear me out just listening to all she did during the day. No matter what she had to do in a day, she always looked beautiful. I believe that summer she was trying to make up for lost time.

She felt like she had to hurry up to try to make things okay again just like they were before she was diagnosed. She had the "guilties," I should say, for not being able to do some of the things that needed to be done while she was in the hospital going through treatments. She had the feeling that it was her fault for having cancer and that she was somehow bad to have had this thing influence her little family's life, turning it upside-down so many times.

It was hard for me to try to turn these feelings around for her. She had had a lifetime of the "guilties" for never being smart enough to make the right decision. I had a lifetime of it, as well as our brothers and sisters. We were always made to feel like we just weren't good enough or important enough or smart enough or whatever. When you live like this as a kid, there are repercussions later in adulthood.

All six of us, at one time or another, experienced obstacles we had to overcome because of the lack of loving, nurturing, unconditional love that most parents embellish on their children. This always bothered all of us but with Nena, it was ever more hurtful, as neither parent had very much to do with her or her little family during this medical crisis in her life, not that there was much contact before all this happened.

All of this wore on sister, and I would try to calm her by reminding her that if she hadn't been treated as she was, she might not be the great mom that she is. "We should all be grateful," I would say. "Look at how we all turned out by doing everything we can *not* to be like them." She would agree, and then we'd talk about all of us and laugh a little, cry a little, and then be happy again. But somewhere, deep down inside, those feelings never go away. I always seem to be second-guessing myself, even to this very day. I know Nena felt the same way.

Denny, Nena, and the boys took that vacation and had a great time. She packed everything but the kitchen sink in the van. Denny and the boys really enjoyed the battlefields and historic places out East. Nena enjoyed being with her boys and husband but secretly said that she was exhausted most of the time.

With autumn approaching again, there was much to do. There were berries and nuts to gather, squash and pumpkins to bake and freeze for holiday cooking, and all the late garden harvesting, as well as school shopping for the boys. She managed all of it. She managed. But all the while, the lump on her chest that never did go away, was growing. Now she also felt one on her back.

The time was drawing near for reevaluation. She was scared. I just kept telling her to be happy that those lumps presented themselves so she could do something about it. Some people are never shown any outside, physical proof; it's inside, where they can't see it, and so they don't know to do anything until it's too late.

Retest

THE DAY HAD COME: our two- to four-day venture back to Zion. Our trip was a good one, with lots of conversation. We always had something to talk about, mostly always about Denny and the boys. But, love them as she did, there were times when the other side of my beautiful sister took over. She could get riled in a heartbeat, and then she could also stay that way.

Cancer feeds on stress, so I would always ask God before our journeys to give me strength and the words to say. He always did. With God's help, I could turn a bad situation into a better one. I would say there's always a reason for everything and it's always for the best, even if it doesn't look like it at the time. Usually, by the time we reached Zion, we'd have solved all the problems in the family and in the world.

We found our hotel room, called for delivery pizza, ate our supper, and went to bed. We were up bright and early, showered, dressed, and headed to the cafeteria for coffee and breakfast. Everyone at the hospital, including the cafeteria people, were happy to see us, and they all remarked about how great Nena looked.

For the next few days, it was test after test. They tested from head to toe and everywhere in between. We'd get through early in the afternoon and drive around looking for garage sales or go to the bargain stores or sometimes just get something to eat and go to the beach at Lake Michigan and sit.

Consultation day was upon us. The doctors already had a plan in place when they explained that the cancer was back. They had a new kind of chemotherapy. They couldn't radiate the chest area again, but with these two new drugs combined, there was hope for a good outcome: if not possible to kill it, to keep it from growing.

Nena lost it. To keep it from growing was not good enough. She would do whatever it took to get rid of it. She didn't want to wait. She wanted a treatment now. It was Friday; they gave her the first treatment and told her to be back on Monday.

All the way home, sister was mad, crying and pissed off because she had to rearrange her life again for this. She had a lot to do over the short weekend, and with all the new, unfamiliar drugs running through her body, she managed just fine.

For the next several months, we spent three or four days a week in Zion doing treatments, making friends, attending group meetings, and just hanging out together. During these months, the staff was discussing a bone marrow transplant with us.

This was another new procedure. Supposedly, by running your blood through this new machine, they could harvest stem cells and, at a later date, reintroduce them back into the body. It would mean thirty days in isolation. The immune system would be totally depleted of anything good, and the possibilities of infection were enormous.

Nena didn't care what it took; she felt that this would be a great backup to this new round of chemotherapy. She thought, *How could cancer continue to grow after all this?* She would consent to the bone marrow transplant; it could be a very complicated process, but she felt she had to do it.

Rearrange Life Again

THEY GAVE HER A month break from appointments and testing. Nena kept busy rearranging her life again. She changed schedules, decided where the boys would stay, cooked, cleaned, shopped, did laundry, and all the other miscellaneous things she needed to do. Other than a few allergic reactions, a couple of emergency room visits, and a few short-term hospital stays, she managed.

The boys were out of school for the summer, and knowing that they were not allowed in the bone marrow unit made her lonely and homesick before she even left.

I began to notice changes in my sister, her attitude, her looks, and her logic. Considering everything she'd already been through, it wasn't hard to understand. She was mad at the whole cancer situation. The excessive amount of drugs and the terrible side effects, or allergic reactions to them, had taken a toll on her beautiful body, not to mention trying to keep a hat on in the wind. Everything aggravated her. She had become even more protective than ever of the boys and was adamant about their care, to whoever would be caring for them. She managed.

Of course, while sister was doing all that she could, I did my part to help by explaining everything as best as I could to our siblings. I had plenty of time to think about this isolation thing so, after the siblings knew everything, we decided to take turns keeping her company.

Any and I would go first and stay a few days. Then I would go back home with Amy and return with Mark; then I'd go back home and return with Scottie. All in all, I think sister was without any of us for four days during her entire stay. Denny, of course, would go as often as he could, as well as a couple of friends that lived close to the hospital.

She could have a few visitors, but it was a rigorous procedure to go inside her room. Everything and everyone had to be as sterile as possible. We had to scrub up, wear boots and masks, sign in, and sign out.

We made the absolute best out of the situation. Amy and I decorated the stark walls in her room with all the things she loved the most. Her sons' pictures, from each year since they were born, hung on the wall directly in front of the bed where she could see them every time she opened those beautiful eyes.

We put up posters of angels and waterfalls and poems. Each day, cards would come to her from family, friends, Denny, and the boys. Amy posted a note in our local newspaper to let everyone know where to send cards. Each day, we would wipe down all the mail with sterilizing cloths so Nena could touch them and read them.

We made sure she had cards of her own to send to Denny and the boys with treats of baseball cards, stickers of all kinds, and sticks of gum to enclose in the cards for her boys. We would always leave her alone when she wrote out her cards. We thought it was a private thing.

We'd play dice with her when she was up to it. Every time one would roll off the bed table, it would have to be sterilized. Whenever Nena was feeling blue, we'd make lighthearted conversation. Sometimes we'd talk about other people's problems, and then hers wouldn't seem so bad.

Each day, we would watch the board to see if her counts were up. After the bone marrow transplant was done, her complete blood count was next to nothing. We waited and waited. Finally, after ten days, they started climbing very slowly.

During this time, she contracted a very bad fungal infection between her toes on one foot. When the immune system is compromised, infections and diseases that have lain dormant for years, surface.

She was having a very difficult time physically, not to mention the isolation and knowing she wouldn't be home in time for Chase's birthday. She didn't feel well; she was lonely and homesick.

One the evening of August 1st, Denny snuck Chase into Nena's room to surprise her. No children were allowed in the ward, but it was just the medicine sister needed. They got to visit together for a short while, and then Denny and Chase left for the journey home.

She survived the bone marrow transplant, but there was still a big concern over the infection in her foot. She could be discharged from the hospital but would have to stay at a hotel and go back and forth each day as an outpatient. She learned how to maneuver with a walker but was still very weak.

I moved us into a rented room across the street from the hospital. It was a great day; she was happy to be out. We rode around so she could smell the fresh air, stopped to eat a drive-in, and headed back to the room. I helped her get ready for bed, propped her up, and made her cozy.

I was about to shower when the phone rang. It was George, and he was in bad pain. He called me earlier at the hospital and told me he had been in severe pain and actually took himself to see a doctor that day. That was highly unusual.

The doctor told him that he had polyps in his colon and that she'd call in a prescription for him. He told me the name of the prescribed drug and assured me that he'd be okay.

The drug he said he picked up was unfamiliar to me, so after I hung up the phone, I went to the hospital pharmacist to ask about this prescription. The pharmacist told me that it was used to combat bad cases of acne. I was furious and very concerned that some quack doctor must have seen George. I knew I had to get home to him, but I was moving my sister out of the hospital.

I explained to sister what happened with George and told her I needed to get back home and take care of him. She agreed and said she'd be all right alone; I adamantly disagreed and immediately called Denny.

Earlier in the evening, Nena needed to use the bathroom and thought she could do it all by herself. Before she even got close to it, I was scrambling to pick her up off the floor. The walker was awkward, and she was still very weak. I was not going to leave her unattended.

I called Denny and told him to leave immediately for Zion and that I'd get someone else to help Nena until he arrived. We met some of our neighbors in the other rented rooms who were also being treated at the hospital. I went to the one I knew the best.

The neighbor woman was with her husband, who also had cancer, but he was asleep and probably would be for hours. I asked her if she could come and tend to my sister until Denny arrived. I said my goodbyes to Nena, who still insisted she'd be all right alone until Denny came. I didn't want to bring it up in front of the neighbor lady, but I reminded by dear sweet, stubborn sister about the little stumble she'd taken "all by herself." We hugged and kissed and cried, and then I got into my care and headed back to Wisconsin in the middle of the night.

I asked for the white light of the Holy Spirit to surround and protect me. I also asked my brother Johnnie to ride along with me, keep me between the lines, and keep my eyes open. I instantly felt a brushing movement against my right arm, as if someone were sitting right next to me. I knew Johnnie would be taking the ride with me, and I thanked him. I talked out loud to him about a lot of things that night, and I just knew he'd heard every word.

My brother Johnnie was the sibling next in line to me. He passed away ten years earlier, after falling out of the tree where he was hanging a tire swing for his two-year-old daughter, Stephanie. Johnnie was thirty-two years old. He had a ten-year-old son named after him who we called John-John and a baby girl named Felicia, who was born a few weeks after we buried him. I missed my brother and longed for him. Whenever I needed help, I always asked him. Tonight, I felt him.

Before long, I was pulling up into my driveway. George was in bed, moaning and sobbing loudly. We got him dressed and headed for the hospital in Madison, seventy miles away, totally bypassing the hospital where he'd been only a few hours earlier. The long trip felt unending for George; the pain was excruciating with every bump in the road.

In the emergency room, a doctor that recognized George from a previous visit met us. He knew, after a short examination, that George had kidney stones that were lodged. He told us that most patients describe these stones as "pain similar to that of childbirth." George said, "I must be having twins!"

Some tests were done, and a room was made available for him. An operation was needed because of where the stones were located. They described the procedure to us; George was glad he'd be sleeping through it.

Shortly after the operation began, the surgeon came to me in the waiting room. The operation was unsuccessful. They had gotten as far as the bladder when they discovered suspicious tumors and backed out. They'd have to try to break up the stones with a sonic blast accomplished with lasers and water. He felt that these tumors, as well as the prostate, needed attention and that George would need to speak to another surgeon after the kidney stone problem was fixed.

On the fourth day, we were able to go home, leaving with some not-so-good news. George was still in tremendous pain.

He was still very upset with the doctor who had misdiagnosed him, so on the way home from the hospital, we stopped at the other hospital, at George's insistence, to revisit that doctor. She was conveniently in a meeting. George got his point across to her nurse and all the people in the waiting room: some doctors shouldn't be practicing medicine.

The machine that would be the stone crusher would be in Madison the following week. The doctors were hoping that, even though painful, George might pass the stones on his own. It would prove to be a very long week.

Meanwhile, Nena was having a very difficult time in Zion. It appeared that all the different drugs she was on for the fungal infection were not working. The infection had gone into her bloodstream.

Later in the evening, the same day I brought George home from the hospital, Nena called me to say that she and Denny were leaving Zion and going to the UW at Madison. They thought they'd feel more confident seeing the infectious disease team in Madison. Zion was afraid that without amputation of the foot Nena's life was in danger in a big way. Nena couldn't stand the thought of losing her foot, so she and Denny left Zion and arrived in Madison in the middle of the night. Nena was sick and tired and hurting.

I was unable to do anything to help her; my heart was so heavy. But I was where I needed to be, and Nena was where she needed to be.

Amy went to the hospital to be with Nena and kept in touch with me by phone. Nena's counts had fallen sharply overnight after leaving Zion. Amy explained to me, after the results from Nena's MRI were in, that they might have to remove the infection in the soft tissues surgically and, once in there, may need to amputate toes. The infection may also have silently moved to other parts of her body, so they would be running many tests. She would also have two to three months of an antibiotic drip, but this could be done at home.

It was also during this time that the insurance started becoming an issue. Their coverage was from the company where Denny worked, and they were preparing to change insurance companies. This issue threatened to disrupt coverage for Nena. It became a very stressful part of the "every day, not knowing for sure" game.

To try to buy insurance for health coverage independently would be fruitless. No insurance company would touch her. I knew, because I tried to do all the same things for George way back when. I also knew that the coverage had to be getting very close to running out for Nena and Denny's workplace still hadn't decided whether to bring in a new insurance company or not.

After several days, the UW Hospital sent my sister home with IVs, shots to give to herself, and a catheter. A home health care nurse would go to Nena's house once a day. She would be alone all day, with all this stuff hooked up to her, while Denny was at work and the boys were at school. It all made me crazy. I secretly wondered if the hospital let her go home like this because she had indeed run herself out of insurance.

While all of this was going on at Nena's, my house was also unbalanced. George had to go back to the emergency room in Madison and was immediately put on mega doses of antibiotics. One of the stones had lodged itself where it became difficult to urinate, and it was backing up inside him. They kept him in the hospital on an IV drip for infection and pain. Two days later the machine would crush those stones, and he was able to pass them. He would never go back for any further appointments to have any of the other areas examined.

Several days had passed before I got to see Nena, and when George and I got to her house, I put on my usual happy face when I saw her. Inside, I ached for her and was so upset to see this situation in a home setting. When I was a kid, you stayed in the hospital for two weeks just for appendectomies. Now you have to be almost stone cold before they keep you any length of time. Whoever heard of going home with hospital things still attached to the inside and outside of your body?

I acted as though this was a perfectly normal thing. I could see that Nena was becoming very knowledgeable about proper flushing of the lines and all the technical stuff. The home health nurses were great to her. They were educating Nena, and she was educating them. Still, it bothered me, and I didn't think she looked good at all.

We spent the day together. George and Nena talked, and I busied myself around her house. I got everything done and had supper dished up when Denny and the boys got home. We left the little family to enjoy each other.

I knew sister would have a good night. We women always feel better when our houses are clean, our laundry is done, and the house smells of down home cooking.

Get A Job

WE SPOKE TO EACH other daily by phone, and George and I visited Nena and her family as often as we could. I went with her to her doctor's appointments, and most of the time now, our sister Amy also went along.

We would make a whole day of it. Amy had a nice comfortable van, so she was the driver. We'd drink coffee all the way to Madison, talking about our lives all the way there. Nena did most of the talking; she always had something to say, mostly complained, but she had good reason. It was hard for her to find the good in anything.

After weeks, then months had passed, Nena was doing better. Also during this time, we found out that there indeed would be problems with the insurance company if something wasn't done soon. The stress was already unbearable, and now she felt responsible for getting a full-time job so she could get benefits, hoping she could find a place that wouldn't require a physical examination first. She found a job.

She didn't care that they were paying her just a little more than minimum wage; all she cared about was that in ninety days, she'd have benefits. Then she'd be able to relax her mind about whether or not Denny's work was changing insurance companies.

She worked in a retail store. She was in charge of several departments and worked harder than any three women that worked there. Constantly on her feet, she was non-stop all day every day. I don't know how she did it. She'd be tired and exhausted when I talked to her. All the things at home that needed her attention she let slide because she didn't have the strength to do it all. Her main concern was the "benefits."

The holidays were drawing near, and Nena wanted to have Christmas dinner for her siblings and their families. We all agreed, even though we didn't like the idea of all the work involved for her. She enjoyed doing it all. It was the first time she got to have her own people at her home for a holiday; she was on an incredible high.

Denny's employer settled the insurance issue, and as it turned out, Nena would be covered under this new plan. So now, she actually had three: his, hers, and social security Medicare. She continued working, doing the mom and wife thing, but was constantly upset with herself that she just couldn't get everything done fast enough.

When she had a day off from her job, I'd visit and help her get caught up with house chores and the laundry. It would always be a great time. Sometimes Denny would pop in and surprise us with a brief visit, just to make sure everything was okay. Sometimes George would come and bring each of us a rose, visit for a while, and then he went home and waited for me to arrive.

Retest and Rearrange

It was now April and time to be retested from head to toe, and we, the three sisters, went together. It was several days of testing, but once the tests were done each day, we'd be three girls looking for something fun to do. We enjoyed each other's company and always had a great time together.

The both of them, so much younger than me, made me feel not only like the older sister, but also in many ways like their mom. On more than one occasion, they have each said that very thing to me.

They'd make me crazy when we'd go shopping because I could never find them. Neither one grew up to be very tall, maybe five foot. I'm five foot six inches tall, trying to scan the clothing department for two brunettes, when they were shorter than the clothes racks. Thinking about it now, I wonder if they tried to lose me on purpose.

When we walked anywhere, they were always ten feet out in front of me, even with their short legs. I loved being with these "little girls" as I always called them. They were as different as day and night, but they loved each other; and I loved them both. Over the years, I grew to admire the woman and mothers they'd become. I've been extremely proud of them and continue to be.

A conference always followed Nena's tests. All the results from the tests taken over the previous days were in on the last day of testing; we never had to wait a long period of time. The doctors came into the room where we waited to hear their findings. There it was. A mass in one lung, perhaps the spots in the other lung were scar tissue or something, but the mass was most definitely a mass.

We had, from the very first day, been involved in doing our own research: getting copies of all tests, reviewing them, and always looking over X-rays. The three of us had become quite good at the whole medical lingo thing, and we knew what we were looking at. It wasn't a pretty picture.

Nena was devastated. She was mad and scared; she didn't want to believe what she was seeing. She was totally overwhelmed by emotion and fear.

The medical staff proposed surgery to remove the sections of lung where the tumor was growing, followed up of course with more chemo and radiation. So the plans and schedules were made.

Nena and Denny checked in at the hospital the day before surgery. We arrived very early the next morning, my brothers, Amy, and me. Nena was so happy; she never expected all the siblings to be there.

Before she was rolled behind the surgical doors, I leaned down and told her that I'd spoken to Johnnie during the night and he told me to tell her that he would be in the operating room and he'd be holding her hand. She told me later it was the last thing she remembered before she zoned out.

Again she came out of surgery with flying colors. She also handled the treatments well, and after only a few weeks, she was back working at the store and continued working while she was going through her treatments.

I had been scheming, behind her back, to make a big to-do of the last day of treatment. She was very surprised. Before she went in for her last treatment, our brothers met us at the hospital. We decided that this would be her last treatment, forever, and we all wanted to be a part of it. Together, the five of us rode the elevator down to the basement, where Nena got her treatment. Afterwards, all five of us went into the doctor's office. The staff wished us well, and we were out the door to enjoy a wonderful lunch together.

Mark had ridden his Harley that day, so he tied a scarf on Nena's head, put a helmet on her, and drove his baby sister the seventy miles back home; it was the ride of her life. I hope my brother knows how much happiness she felt that day with her special ride home with her favorite brother.

The sibling bond between us all was great, but the bond that was held separately between the three oldest and the three youngest was also strong, a force in itself to be reckoned with. It all had its connection. With no disrespect intended, each of us had our favorites or ones we were even closer to. I was always the one that made out the best; being the oldest, most definitely, had its rewards. I've known them all since the day they were born; I've been exceptionally blessed with these siblings.

With her last treatment behind her, it was business and life as usual. She didn't realize at the time, however, that the treatments were catching up to her. She didn't feel good, didn't feel right, and she began to have a constant noise in her head and ears. She finally agreed to take a leave of absence from her job and, shortly thereafter, had her first seizure in the front yard of her home.

Siblings Stand United

DENNY WAS THERE WHEN it happened and called 911. He called me after that, and I met them at the emergency room of the local hospital. They let me in to see her; behind the curtain there she laid, eyes closed. When I bent down over her, she opened those beautiful blue eyes. The fear I saw in them was beyond describable words. She began to cry as she pulled me down to her.

"I thought I was dying, sister. I was so scared! I don't want to die, Nanc."

I'll never forget those words. With all my strength, I told her everything was going to be just fine.

These doctors, in the local ER, were in touch with the staff at UW in Madison about Nena's seizure. They gave her some pills and made an appointment for the following day, back in Madison. They explained that this sometimes happens after treatments; but they would give her seizure medicine, and that should take care of it. They sent us home with Dilantin.

We are, unfortunately or fortunately, somewhat educated about seizures and this medicine because our brother Mark has been treated for epilepsy for many years. We know how difficult it is to keep this drug regulated in your system to be able to control seizures.

I was very nervous about all this seizure stuff. It was such a long way to Madison, especially in the middle of the night, if something would go wrong. We went to Madison the following day. The doctors there explained when and how much Dilantin to take. I didn't like it.

She seemed to be doing pretty well after a few days of taking this medicine but would still get seizures. With each new seizure, they increased the medicine. Then she started not feeling so good again.

I went by one morning; Nena was on the couch all curled up, looking very pale and holding her chest. She opened her shirt to show me the redness; it appeared to me to be one big, giant hive. She explained to me how she'd been doing; then I glanced back at the hive. It appeared to be growing right in front of my eyes.

I quickly got a tape and measured the area, jotting down the numbers as I was calling the oncology staff in Madison. By the time someone came to the phone, and as I explained what was going on, it had grown and was starting up her neck. We made a few necessary phone calls, got in the car, and drove as fast as I could to Madison. They were ready for her when we arrived and began pumping her full of "whatever," totally baffled about its cause. She had been taking Dilantin for several weeks at this time. By the time they figured out that it was an allergic reaction to the Dilantin, sister was very swollen.

I called Amy at work shortly after I got Nena to the hospital. I told her everything that had happened and that I felt she needed to come. Amy left work and went straight to Nena's bedside. Nena was so happy to see her. We waited for the staff to get Nena a room as we continued to watch this new rash cover her.

The reaction had done absolutely horrific things to her body. The scientists at the hospital asked her if she'd permit them to take pictures of her to study. She agreed. They took pictures of her distorted, deformed looking body. I wanted to rip their heads off. Silently.

I called Denny at work, after we found out all the details, and told him I wouldn't be bringing her home that night. I also called the brothers, told them they needed to come as soon as possible and that they needed to make the necessary arrangements to stay. Nena needed us, and she needed all of us. Nena was very scared.

The care she required at the time would be intense, and because we would only accept the best care for her, we needed to be there; we were the best and we knew it. The brothers were there that day and knew they needed to stay with us; we all needed each other. The first few days there, Nena seemed to be getting worse.

We did everything for her medically, physically, mentally, spiritually, and emotionally. We took turns lying in bed with her, holding her, and giving her comfort. We cleaned her, tended to her open sores, and gently massaged her. We even made a big deal out of every meal.

I sat silently several times in that room just feeling the love and tender nurturing that filled the room, like the sweet smell of jasmine. All for the love of sister. Nena made it very clear to us that she wanted no one to see her like this, under any circumstances.

We had a sibling discussion about what she said after she fell asleep. When Denny arrived, we told him what was said. The siblings and Denny made the decision to take whatever steps necessary to prevent any calls or visitors to sister during this hospital stay.

Security was involved and people's feelings were hurt over the whole deal, but we had become very protective of our baby sister. If that's the way she wanted it, that's the way it would be. She was perfectly content to have only Denny and her siblings by her side.

It proved to be quite a week, but she would eventually heal at home and of course, change medicines. It was a slow, painful recovery for her and had taken its toll. But over all, she was doing great.

Making Memories

IT WAS EARLY MAY. George and I were throwing a party to celebrate paying off the mortgage on our house, not an easy task when you're on disability. He was obsessed with paying it off; he'd double or triple the payments every month. It wasn't easy, but we did it.

Nena, Denny, and the boys were the first to arrive. The boys made their plates and sat on the stoop to eat with Aunt Virg, George's sister from Chicago. George and Nena sat at the table; I knew she needed to speak privately with him.

Denny and I went outside to have one of our open and honest talks. I told him he should take this summer to make some memories. I told him that I felt this cancer would travel to the brain and that I didn't feel that sister would see her next birthday. He listened, but I knew that it sure wasn't easy to hear, let alone say. My track record about different things along the way was almost to detail, and Denny knew it.

Inside, George and Nena talked alone quietly. I later found out that Nena was asking George about dying. George assured her that the worst thing in life was not death. George and Nena had a common bond, a bond that brings dying people to a level where no one else can possibly be unless they've been there. I can only imagine the depths of their private conversations.

Nena trusted George. He filled many roles for her. Not only was he her brother-in-law, but she considered him to be her brother. He was older and wiser. She found parental qualities in him as well as a great friendship, not to mention the dreaded disease they had in their bodies that kept them in tune to each other. They definitely felt each other's pain, unlike the rest of us. I'm so grateful they had each other in their lives.

The party was great. George and I actually took the loan papers and tossed them into the fire pit, and everyone celebrated with a toast. Our family, friends, neighbors, and bank officers were with us. It was a feeling unlike any other for George and I to know that, together, we had done this. We were happy for so many reasons, and to share this moment with the people we loved was fabulous.

I cooked all Italian food, of course; maybe I didn't mention that George is Italian. Over the years, I mastered the art of his favorite cooking, and it became a family tradition for me to cook for both sides of the family. This dinner was no different than what my siblings did when they threw a party. One thing's for sure, not only does this family work hard, but we play and party hard too.

Life seemed good for me, but always lurking in the shadows of my very being, lingered this feeling. My love and concern for my husband and sister was so intense, it seemed no matter which direction I turned, there was death and dying. I knew good and well I would handle it, no matter what, and I would stay strong for everyone. I couldn't ever let anyone see me sweat, so I bucked it up, prayed a lot, and asked for help when I needed it—guidance, wisdom, and knowledge. I constantly prayed for the right words to come to me in any given situation. I asked and I received. Always.

On several occasions, during dreamtime, different answers or visions would come to me, often without asking. It was one of those visions that made me call my brother Mark one morning after I awoke.

I needed to find out at what angle the sun would set at the cemetery where our brother was buried. I was told during dreamtime that we should go to his grave and have a sibling picture taken; it would be the last time that all six of us could be in the same photo because Nena soon would be miles away in a different cemetery. I was told how we all should dress, that there needed to be red flowers placed at Johnnie's grave, and that Barbara should take the pictures.

Markie told me what I wanted to know, and I began making the plans. I called my siblings and invited them and their families to our house for Sunday spaghetti dinner the following weekend. My siblings were to wear blue jean colored shirts. I didn't tell Nena the "whys" of the pictures, just that we all thought it was a great idea. She was all up for it. Barbara was thrilled to be asked to be our photographer for the day, and I just happened to have pots of beautiful red geraniums on my front stoop to take along.

All the families arrived that day with their wonderful hearty appetites. After we finished off a twenty-two-quart Nesco full of sauce and meatballs, the siblings and Barbara got into the van and headed out. The others stayed behind and did the cleanup and waited for us to return.

It was a great trip to the cemetery, and once we were there, it got even better. We all had such a good time. We cleaned and polished the headstone and placed the red geraniums at the sides of the stone, toward the front.

Barbara snapped several different shots as we playfully posed for the camera. Nena didn't have a lot of hair, so Mark brought along one of his red, fox skin hats for her to wear. There was lots of laughter and almost child-like behavior. It was a good time, and I was so grateful.

Yes, I knew it would be the last time we, all six siblings, would be represented in a photo together, but I was so grateful that we were there doing what we were doing; everyone else was, too.

After all the pictures were taken, we said our prayers around our brother's marker and piled back into the van. We took the long way home, riding down the backcountry roads that some of us hadn't been on since we were kids riding the school bus. Many stories got told along the way that day; even some secrets. It truly had been an awesome day.

The pictures were developed later in the week; we were all so happy with the results. The sunlight was just right as it cast down in late afternoon over all of us. Rolling hills and cornfields were our backdrop. Considering the circumstances, I will always cherish the memory of that day through our very touching pictures.

Brother Scottie was busy planning a cousin's reunion party, which would bring us all together, possibly to be with Nena for the last time. Cousins from all over the country would be there. Nena didn't know it had anything to do with her, and she never did. It was a weekend party that would take place following Nena's next doctor's appointment. We all had our jobs to do to pull this off. Everything was set and ready, with only last-minute preparations to be done.

Nena had a doctor's appointment the day before the cousins' reunion. Denny took her because I was preparing for the weekend celebration. Nena said she'd call when she got through with the appointment. As we were putting on the last minute touches at Scottie's place, Denny and Nena drove in. I knew it was not good news.

Nena told us what the doctors said; the brain scan showed several tumors. It was the worst news. Scottie held her briefly as she wept; all of us took turns hugging her. Denny and Nena stayed only briefly and then left for their home. She spoke to everyone that night, over the phone, and assured us she would still be at the party. We all had to put this news somewhere, anywhere; we could not let this dampen the party spirit.

The weather the next day was absolutely perfect. Amy, the boys, and I greeted all the cousins as they arrived. We quickly explained the latest news as they got out of their cars and asked them not to mention it again for the rest of the weekend. And that's how it was, unless sister wanted to talk about it; and she didn't!

It was a party unlike any I'd ever been to. We did pull this off and in a really big way. We had a huge beer tent set up and hung Christmas lights on the inside for when it got dark, and that's where we had all the food and drink. It was a perfect setup.

We cooked a hog, deep fried twelve chickens, and roasted two turkeys; that was just the meat. We had buffet tables, butted end-to-end four tables long, filled with food that everyone brought, and Nesco roasters filled with cowboy potatoes and Aunt Nanc's baked beans. The food was exceptional. Our family has an incredible appetite for good food, good people, and a good time.

Our sister-in-law, Cat, had all the proper connections when it comes to throwing a party like no one else can afford to throw. Without her knowing whom she knew, we wouldn't have had all the toys and baubles we got to play with. She also managed to bring two gators that could go anywhere, and I mean anywhere; John Deere makes them with six wheels.

My young nephews cut trails through the property with chainsaws that took you through a small creek, passing through thick, green foliage on each side, steep hills with ruts and twists and turns that simply took your breath away. The kids had simply outdone themselves; they thought the trails were perfect. They asked me to ride the trail with them to be sure. As we rode along, if I saw a low branch or anything in the way, they took care of it with the chainsaw. They did a fine job; it was definitely ready for family entertainment. Those six-wheelers and that trail were in use every waking moment, all weekend.

When it was my turn to drive, I loaded up my girls (Amy, Nena, and four of our female cousins, all about the girls' age) and a few bottles of some very wonderful locally-made wine. We strapped a life jacket on Nena, just for fun, told her to hang on to her hair (wig), and away we went. I don't know when I laughed that hard or if I ever did. I'd stop every now and then, long enough to pass the bottle around, and then we'd be off again to see what was around the next corner. All the girls were laughing, crying, and holding on; it was so much fun.

We came down a very steep hill and entered peacefully into an open meadow; it actually turned out to be somebody's yard. Trees on three sides hid this gorgeous A-frame house, set back on a hill. There was a patio to one side with a picnic table and a few lounge chairs. The backdrop was beautiful; I thought what a great picture that would be.

No one was home, and considering the circumstances, we really didn't think anyone would mind if we drove up to the house and took a picture. Certainly, if this place were ours and some sweet, all-American girls wanted to do this sort of thing, we wouldn't have a problem with it; and that's just what we did. We parked the six-wheeler in a position so that Amy could adjust the camera and jump up on the porch to be in the picture before the camera shutter clicked.

We stayed and enjoyed that brief moment on that porch, acting like the devilish little girls who really got away with something. I watched my sisters and my young cousins, now all grown up and beautiful; my heart was proud to know the feeling of this kind of sisterhood. We loaded back up and made our way back, all of us different than when we left. The feeling of being together again, all grown up with lives, families, and issues of our own, yet all of us still very much the same as when we were kids.

All the girls were much younger than me, and it gave me great pleasure to see the way these beautiful, young women had turned out. For a while, at least, we enjoyed each other's company and the freedom we felt and the love that enclosed us like a bubble. It's a secure feeling knowing that relationships, built during childhood days, carry on forever in families. Our sibling bond had remained strong over the years, and the bond we share with many of our cousins is equally as strong.

We had a huge bonfire that evening that burned for several days afterwards. There was not one person that didn't have the very best time of any other reunion they'd ever been to. Everything had been a huge success, and we were all pleased; we all got to escape the real world for a weekend.

Denny and Nena and the kids had to attend the company picnic the following day at the place where Nena had worked. She was really looking forward to it and said she'd call me when they got home.

She called early that evening and indeed, had a wonderful time, but the trip home was even more wonderful. She explained that as they were turning onto the gravel road that runs past their house, she noticed clouds in the sky that were shaped like Johnnie, our brother, and our grandparents and uncle, who had also passed. Upon seeing this, Nena said she felt like it was a sign, a sign that meant this brain thing was going to be fixed and that the cancer was going to be gone.

She talked on and on, and I just let her. She'd been so taken by the whole experience, and when she asked me what I thought about it, I just said that I thought she'd had a vision and they were telling her that everything is going to be fine. That's what I felt, but Nena's interpretation and mine were quite different, as was the case so many times during this battle with cancer.

I kept my view inside and would tell sister over and over, from time to time, that everything would be just fine; that's what I truly believed. This is not, however, how Nena heard it. So that's the way it was.

Privately, I knew that this was a sign for me to recognize; a sign from my brother. I knew his spiritual presence was closer, now more than ever. I felt very happy knowing he was hanging with us, and I knew more signs would be forthcoming. I prayed for strength, guidance, wisdom, and the right words to speak, and to help me remain keenly aware.

We went back to Madison for the doctors to propose the new plan. Nena's course of treatment for the brain tumors was called "whole head radiation." These words cut through me like a knife. Nena wanted whatever was needed to fix this. And so they proceeded to radiate the head and brain. Nena was in a room with steel plated doors; it had lasers and machines of all kinds waiting to do very unnatural things to a person's body.

Amy and I would speak privately to Nena's radiation doctors with up-close-and-personal conversations. We didn't want to know a bunch of crap; we just wanted to know! The prognosis, of course, was not good, and when the doctors tried to explain to Nena about the chances of death, she absolutely refused to hear it, believe it, or acknowledge it in any way.

The holidays were quickly approaching, so Amy and I made sure that Nena got to do all the shopping she wanted to, even though she was totally exhausted after each treatment. We watched, over the next couple of weeks, as sister started to slip in many ways; her thinking was foggy, her pace had slowed, and overall, she just wasn't doing well.

Getting all the right things for her boys for Christmas meant everything to her. I remember walking through this little strip mall, the two little girls walking ten feet in front of me, as usual. Amy paced herself to Nena's gait, which was more and more becoming only a shuffle. The mall was beautifully decorated for the holidays; trees adorned one end of the mall to the other, all decorated differently; music piped in all around, and garland and tinsel hung overhead.

I stopped and quickly hid behind one of the beautiful Christmas trees and just sobbed. I knew I was watching those two little girls walk together, ten feet in front of me, Christmas shopping for the last time. That thought totally wrecked me. I allowed myself to cry, pulled myself back together, and caught up with the girls. They never knew.

Help From Beyond

LATE ONE NIGHT THE phone rang, startling me into extreme awareness. My "self" was trained and programmed for immediate response. When I answered, to my surprise, it wasn't someone from Nena's house calling, but my brother's son, John-John. A lot of nieces and nephews called late at night for private talks with Aunt Nanc or Uncle George, so this wasn't unusual.

His tone of voice was shaky and sounded as though he had been crying. I remained calm as he began to tell me that he just woke up from a bad dream: a bad nightmare. I asked him to try to remember every detail and then tell it to me.

He began by saying that it happened in his apartment in Idaho. He said, "You were all there: you, Uncle Scott, Uncle Mark, and Aunt Amy. You were in here and taking all my stuff. You were throwing out everything I own, throwing things from the windows and out the doors, and you were all laughing about it. I was begging you to stop, but you didn't; then you just left. As I was running down the steps after you, I saw Dad's old pickup in the parking lot. When he saw me, he started driving toward me. I wanted to be near him, but as I got closer, it seemed like he was aiming the truck at me, like he wanted to run me down. He drove faster toward me, chasing me as I ran away from him, and then I woke up."

He wanted to know why his Dad would want to run him over and why his elders would disrespect his belongings and him like that. The boy was really shaken, and I told him that it couldn't mean anything as bad as he was thinking.

I needed some time to process this myself, and I promised that I would return his call as soon as I could. I told him not to worry about this because I was sure of one thing: my brother, Johnnie, was definitely trying to get a message through to us, and I needed time to put it all together.

I worked through it all that night by doing a special prayer ceremony, meditating, and just listening. By early morning, I returned my nephew's call. I was so happy and excited to tell this sweet boy that the beautiful vision he had, through dreamtime, was loaded with messages. There were many messages, and they were all from his father.

I concluded that it was his dad's way of telling us that he was needed somewhere else, other than Idaho. The aunts and uncles, including myself, were showing him that no matter what, when family needs family, you give up everything. "Everything" now was being represented by material possessions.

Material things are just that—only material things. They aren't the things that matter or last. They have no feelings or true meaning. Tossing out the possessions and laughing about it shows that it doesn't hurt to let things go. I felt the message was quite clear.

His dad, chasing him in the parking lot meant, to me, that his dad was pushing him to get going, to follow the elders, follow the aunts and uncles. I reasoned that his Aunt Nena was not in the dream because she was the one that needed the family, surrounded by her blood family, her lifetime family.

I explained that this was a sign from brother Johnnie to show, maybe a representation of himself through his son's physical presence. I told John-John that there were some things I didn't understand about the vision yet, but I felt he really needed to understand his Aunt Nena's condition.

a Sibling's Story

I told him everything. I always tried to keep everyone up to date about my sister's health. If you really wanted to know the truth, all you had to do was ask, and that's what you would get. The truth.

I rarely went into detail about Nena's condition, other than with family, but I may have unconsciously eased my nephew from a lot of the details. Now he needed to know all the things concerning his Aunt Nena's health. I expressed my feelings that my sister would be joining my brother and that it would be soon. I told him he needed to come home; somehow, some way, he needed to put his life on hold in Idaho and return home to Wisconsin and be prepared to stay with the family for as long as it took.

I truly believed he was shown a sign, for whatever reason, and that he should be quick to make his plans. I told him to notify his employer, his landlord, and his friends that he'd return when he returned. I could say no more.

The information I gave to him was his to do with as he pleased. But, knowing him as I did, I knew he'd be coming home soon. I told him he'd be different the next time he returned to Idaho.

Through my nephew's dream vision, I was able to reaffirm my connection with my brother. Johnnie would have known that his son would come straight to me with something like this, that I'd be able to analyze it for John-John and that it would assure me that he heard my every word and that he was there to help with whatever he could.

I had been talking to him for months about sister's denial and fear of death and dying. I had prayed, meditated, and had a ceremony with some outside help to enable me to help my sister face crossing over. Johnnie's help was what I desperately needed, and this was a confirmation for me that he was working with me through John-John.

I spent the next day at Nena's house doing house stuff. I told her that I had talked to John-John and he was asking about her; he wanted her to know that he loved her.

While driving home, my mind was doing its usual "at the races," as some people call it. All of a sudden, all the lights in the car flashed on for only a second; it got really bright. Just as quickly, another message flashed in my mind about John-John's dream. It all happened in the blink of an eye, just as they say.

My nephew needed to be here; he would be able to help his Aunt Nena accept death. He would be able to show her through his goodness and kindness and gentle nature that kids really do grow up to be fine outstanding people, in spite of having only one parent to raise them. It was all very clear to me now. The only person who could approach her from this direction was John-John.

This was Nena's top priority. Her boys. She couldn't imagine not raising her boys. They were her everything, and it was unacceptable to her that anyone else could raise her sons, only her and Denny. Not one without the other; it wouldn't get done properly. They'd miss out on so much if she didn't do all the things she did for all of them. She didn't believe that one parent was enough. It would be through her nephew's eyes that she would finally come to terms with this.

The vision I had stayed with only me for a while. I knew I would use this information later and share it when it needed to be shared. I knew my sister would be shown a sign, somehow, to give her peace about her sons and their lives.

Nena's radiation treatments lasted longer and longer each session. After each treatment, her head was so hot and red. She was having more and more noises in her head since she started these treatments; she described them as "deafening and unbearable." The seizures also continued.

The radiation department made a mask for her that looked like something from *Star Wars*. The mask was for her entire head. It was to prevent the radiation from going where it shouldn't go. It also helped to make her lie very still. She was strapped down on the table with tie down straps across her head, chest, hips, and feet. It would make me crazy to see her lying there, then to leave her as they closed the doors to make their magic light penetrate her head.

A few days later, John-John arrived home and, shortly afterwards, came over to our house. It was a Thursday night. George and I were happy to see him. I told him he could hang out with all his aunties the following day; it was his Aunt Nena's treatment day. He thought that would be great and agreed to go.

He and uncle did the usual "eating anything and everything" in the kitchen. This included anchovies and celery, to start, and many other things too numerous to mention. To top it all off of course, they had ice cream straight out of the bucket, eaten with a fork.

Uncle taught the kids lots of things over the years, beginning at their birth, or at least when they all became someone he could walk with and talk to. He taught them all about the really meaningful and important things; part of that education was in the eating department. He made connoisseurs out of all of them. John-John, now twenty-something years old, was still sitting with Uncle, eating ice cream with a fork. I loved watching them. I wondered how many, if any, more times they'd have together like that.

I could see John-John's concern for his uncle's breathing. His uncle had gotten worse since he had last seen him. The labored breaths were hard for all of us to hear and see, but for the kids it seemed much harder. He never "went there" with Uncle; he knew others had tried, and he also knew his uncle. Uncle was going to do everything he could without any help, for as long as he could. He didn't want anyone to worry about him, although everyone did, especially the kids. John-John just enjoyed his time with his special Uncle.

I was getting comfortable in my recliner when the phone rang. When I picked up the phone, I could hear my sweet baby *sister* screaming in the background while Denny was saying that

I needed to be there; Nena was calling for me. The pain and fear I heard in my sister's scream was so haunting; I felt so helpless.

All three of us got into my car, and like a crazed woman with beads in one hand and a steering wheel in the other, I quickly drove a thirty-minute trip in half the time. My husband and nephew could only hang on and pray.

Nena had another seizure and was very scared. When we got there, she was somewhat better, but her fear was overwhelming. We medicated her, and I held her as she drifted to sleep for a few hours. George and John-John went back to our house, while I stayed with Nena overnight. I asked George to call Amy and have her pick us up at Nena's in the morning. John-John decided to stay with Uncle, and that pleased me.

During the night, when Nena woke up, she saw me there and decided that she wanted to talk. She spoke openly about her fear of not being able to raise the boys, her fear that no one would be able to love Denny as much as she did, and her fear of being fearful. She was afraid that if she said these things or thought these things, that she really would die; she would be jinxed. I could only say, as I had said so many times before, "Everything will be okay. It will be for the best." It was a heartfelt night.

Morning came, Denny was off to work, the boys were out the door catching the school bus, and I helped sister get ready to go to Madison.

Last Trip to the Hospital

WE WAITED FOR AMY to pick us up; it was Nena's last treatment, and she was happy about that. I knew deep down that this treatment would be out of the question; it was obvious that her blood counts would be very low. I wondered how Nena would accept not being treated. She was not well at all.

This situation was playing hell with my head and my heart to see her continuing to waste the valuable time she had left by insisting on having these treatments. Hours were spent on the road driving back and forth, waiting in line for radiation treatments that were burning holes in her brain and God only knows where else, when she could be spending whatever time she had left enjoying her sons and being with them. Nena thought she had forever.

The three sisters made the best of the long trip to the hospital that morning. Nena was not good, and she was fighting hard to feel better. During the ride to the hospital, she took her medication several times, which was unusual. She was so exhausted from the night before and still shaken, but the drugs did help.

While we were pulling into the parking lot for the "radiation people," I asked Nena if she thought it would be all right for me to go in first and bring out a wheelchair for her. Several times before we had offered, and each time she'd bark back, saying she was fine and that she didn't need a wheelchair. This time, she willingly agreed, so Amy drove up to the door and I brought out a wheelchair.

We waited for Amy to park the van and rode the elevator down together. Nena was still in the wheelchair, not demanding that she could walk; she could hardly hold her head up, let alone walk.

The lab work needed to be done first; they called her name, drew her blood, and then we headed through the length of the hospital, down the elevator to the basement level, and waited in our usual little cubbyhole while sister stayed in her chair.

Nena sat there, so proud that she was getting her last treatment, knowing that this series of treatments fixed the cancer. My heart was breaking inside, and I knew that Amy's had to be, also.

The staff came out and told us that she could not have a treatment because her counts were too low. We needed to leave the Radiation Department and go back up to oncology to talk to those doctors. So we did.

Nena was upset. She needed something to stop this cancer, even if she couldn't have a treatment. She was so sick, so angry; you could see fear radiating throughout her body.

During the consultation, the doctor was called out of the room. Nena started talking, and I excused myself to go to the bathroom. I used this as an excuse to talk to the doctor before he came back into the room.

As he entered the nurses' station, he saw me waiting and called me over to an area to speak with him. He asked very specific questions with answers he knew Nena would not give honestly because of her fears.

He had not seen Nena in a few weeks because she was having radiation treatments, and, of course, that's under another doctor's care. After he looked at the counts on the lab reports and I told him about all the episodes she had since he saw her last, he became quite alarmed. He also sensed Nena's determination for a cure, anything that would make this cancer just go away.

He explained what happens inside the body in Nena's "stage." He told me what to expect and what to look for. Time was most precious now, and he couldn't recommend any further treatment, but he knew my sister was adamant about fixing this cancer thing. I believe, at that moment, he truly felt compassion. He asked me to go back into the room, saying that he'd be there shortly, and not to mention our little talk.

When I entered the room, Amy was holding Nena as she cried, speaking calmly and caressing her. Nena knew this was bad news that her counts were too low for a treatment. A few minutes passed, and while we were trying to pull ourselves together, the doctor came back in.

In a most calming voice, he explained to my sister that her counts had fallen sharply since the last lab tests were done. He told her that chances were high for reoccurring seizures. He could write a script for the onset of seizures; she never gave him a chance to complete his "speech."

Nena responded by insisting on rescheduling the treatment for the following week. It was as if she never heard a word he said. Nena was determined to do everything she could to get her counts back up for the following week's treatment.

Her doctor gave us medication to take home with us, to be given at the onset of the seizures, and a schedule of medications to be taken at a regimented time.

During our conversation in the hallway, the doctor asked me about hospice. I asked him not to use that word in front of my sister. She feared that word, and I didn't want her to have that idea haunting her, along with the rest of the news he had given her.

I assured him that her family would be here for her and that if we needed hospice, I would make the call. He told me to feel free at any time to call the oncology department, day or night, with any questions we might have. He spoke highly about Nena's family and how grateful he was to be part of such an extraordinary caregiving team.

When we left the hospital that day, I prayed that it would be the last time my sister had to ever be there. I had watched, for five years, as cancer had slowly taken her life. She had done everything that modern medicine could offer: put her body, mind, and soul through countless invasive procedures and had allowed things to be done to her that only a woman of her strength could endure. As much as I didn't want to give up hope, I knew that my sister was nearing the end of her life on this realm.

Amy brought the van around to the hospital door, and Nena climbed into the back. She was so tired that she thought she could sleep on the ride home. There was no stopping to have our usual lunch out or go shopping.

It was a very long ride home. Amy and I talked, but very softly. When we talked about our precious sister, we actually wrote notes and did not speak.

Denny and the boys were home when we arrived. Amy took the boys in the living room while Nena sat down at the table and explained to Denny what the doctor said. Nena had a hard time remembering everything that was said, so I filled in the blanks, also explaining about the injections and the medication schedule.

We helped Denny set it all up and made room in the refrigerator for the drugs. I was very nervous about leaving them, but Nena and Denny assured us they'd be fine, and Denny understood the injection procedure. Amy and I left with the understanding that if they needed anything at all, they were to call.

When Amy and I got into the van to go home, I told her about the conversation I had with Nena's doctor in the hallway. We both knew that anything could happen at this point and that we should be prepared to handle whatever came our way. We were doing that all along, but now it would become a bigger challenge. Amy dropped me off at my house, and now I had to tell George all about the day's events.

The Last Ten Days

GEORGE HADN'T SEEN OR talked to me since the previous night, and I felt bad that I didn't have a chance to call him. His breathing had become more labored all summer. He was so sure that when the seasons changed to fall and winter, the humid conditions would also change, and that it would be better. That didn't happen. Anxiety and stress made it even worse.

I was so torn all the time: my husband, my sister; my sister, my husband. Many times, especially that year, I didn't know which one I would lose first.

As I told George the events of the day, he could only cry. He loved her so much, and he knew that I knew: time would be short for Nena. He knew I would do whatever I could for Nena and her family, just as I had always done.

He was glad to have me home for now, and he made me a bowl of Mrs. Grass's Chicken Soup. Whenever he wanted to impress me, he'd cook this box of soup; it was the only thing he could cook, and he did it well. After we ate, he made me lay down for a while; he wanted me rest.

I had only been home a few hours when the phone rang. Denny said that Nena had had another seizure, and it was a bad one. It happened in the bathroom, and she was still in there. He had given her a shot and it helped, but he couldn't get her up off the floor. Denny asked me to come.

George wasn't doing very well, so I told him I was going there alone and that I would call as soon as I could to let him know how things were. We kissed each other goodbye; he said he would pray for Nena and for all of us. He told me to be brave and to just handle it.

I prayed as I drove, calling upon all my angels, "Please let her be alive when I get there; please, God, don't let my sister die on the bathroom floor." I can remember my prayer and asking Johnnie to help me arrive safely, but I can't remember actually driving the distance to her house. I arrived safely, but it was not "I" that drove that little red car.

When I walked into the house, I saw only feet on the floor in the doorway of the bathroom: Nena's feet and Denny's feet. I took a few more steps and saw that he was cradling her in his arms. She looked at me and started to cry.

I knelt down and held them both while Nena cried; we were all scared. Denny and I gently rocked her in our arms and told her everything would be all right. Nena had no strength, and Denny couldn't help her on his own, so together we got her back on the toilet seat where she wanted to be.

She said she was sleepy and wanted a pillow. I set her up with a pillow to lean her head on against the wall and draped a blanket over her lap. I got a chair and sat next to her, touching her, holding her as she drifted in and out. Denny brought another pillow in and lay on the bathroom floor next to us.

Nena drifted in and out of sleep all night. When she finally woke up, we were right there. She didn't feel like she could leave the bathroom, so we told her that she didn't have to and made her as comfortable as we could. She had become very weak physically, and I knew she was not thinking clearly.

Denny was up and down all night, stoking the fire, busying himself, checking up on us in the bathroom, and waiting for morning to arrive so he could get the boys off to school without them having to see their mom in the condition she was in. I stayed with Nena in the bathroom while Denny got the boys ready for school and got them out the door.

Denny had a chance, while getting the boys ready, to call his daughter and her boyfriend to come and help. Nena wanted to go into the front room, but she was not able to walk at all. I was not strong enough to help Denny move her, so I had Denny and Jason make a chair, locking their arms together, and they carried her into the other room. It worked, but Nena felt pain and discomfort. Once we got her into her favorite chair and got her as comfortable as possible, she asked for her shot. We started keeping an accurate chart of medication and dosages given because it was so frequent now.

After she finally fell asleep, I called Amy. I told her where I had been all night and what had happened; she needed to come. Nena could no longer be cared for by Denny alone, and there should be at least three people here at all times. She said she would be right there.

Denny and I had talked about her care, and he agreed that he wouldn't be able to do this alone. He also agreed that Nena would have no part of hospice and that we, the family, would care for her. I asked him for his permission to take over his house, around the clock, for care from my siblings for our sister; he agreed.

Before it was time for the next shot, Nena already needed it, so Denny gave it to her. It was obvious to me that this disease would soon take my sister's life; the progression was rapid.

When Amy arrived, Nena had already fallen back to sleep. I took Amy into another room and told her everything that Denny and I had discussed. I asked her to call the boys; it was time for all the siblings to gather around baby sister and care for her and her family, in these last days. She agreed and made the calls.

Markie hung a "Closed for Family Emergency" sign on the door at the store, turned the key, and left for Nena's house. Scottie told his boss about the call; his boss laid him off so he could be gone for whatever length of time it took. He left immediately for the three-hour drive to Nena's. Nena was so happy; every time she opened her eyes, another sibling was there.

Before long, the little boys arrived home from school. Although Chase and Cole Jesse were happy to have their aunts and uncles there, they sensed change. We all tried to act normal and be fun-loving for the boys, but they knew something was up.

Nena just wanted her sons near her, on her, inside her. Her need and desire was so intense because she loved them so much. I believe she knew the situation had changed and she was losing her grip.

We did everything together after we "moved in." We did anything that needed to be done: a family effort. Everyone excelled at something. When we needed to talk to each other about Nena, we'd go out on the porch so the conversations were away from her and private.

I made several calls that day, back and forth with the hospital. I wanted to make sure we were doing everything right for sister. They reassured me that we were; I gave Amy, the brothers, and Denny any updates concerning hospital consultations.

Someone was always with Nena. It became very obvious in a short period of time that "noise" was more than sister could bear. The sound of the microwave beeping two rooms away hurt her head. Everyone started speaking just above a whisper, and we all started walking lightly across the floor. When the phone rang, we'd answer while we stretched the cord to the porch to talk. I usually answered, as I came to be the liaison between the hospital and the house.

Nena was able to move about the house, with my brothers making her a chair with their arms and carrying her like a princess wherever she needed to go, usually from her recliner to the bathroom, or to the table and back to her recliner. The trips were short, and my brothers insisted that they were honored to carry their baby sister around in their arms whenever she started feeling bad that they had to do that. She couldn't stand the thought of being a burden; we were all so honored to be there with her.

Her body ached all the time, but the pressure she felt inside her head was the worst part. We did everything we could do to accommodate that problem without letting Nena know. We would talk and carry on, laughing about whatever, only in a whisper. Nena was listening, hearing us as though we were speaking out loud.

We gave the meds as scheduled, but it was becoming clear that we'd have to change our plans soon. Someone was always with Nena, while the other were either talking in the kitchen or spending time with the little boys. It was a good system, and we were all happy to be together; eating, taking care of chores, and sleeping next to one another, always within earshot from Nena.

Everyone took his or her shifts, but I stayed awake; I couldn't make myself sleep. I had several sleepless nights before this began, and still I wasn't able to shut my eyes. I watched. I listened. I prayed. I wanted to get everything straight in my head. All things had to be just right. I prayed for my sister's passing to be gentle and loving; I prayed that all the things that could happen to a disease-ridden body during this time not happen. I prayed for strength, and I prayed for my family.

I called George during the night to let him know how everything was progressing. I needed to be at home, caring for him, and I couldn't, and wouldn't, leave my sister. I tried not to let this make me crazy, but the truth is that it tugged at my heartstrings.

Someone else was usually awake also, and we'd end up discussing what to expect next and what alternatives we'd have during any given situation. There was always a constant plan in motion.

The following morning, we got the boys off to school while their mom watched through the large windows, sitting in her recliner. She was so grateful that Amy had read to Cole Jesse before he went to bed and that the boys got their baths and had done their homework without all the usual fuss. She was happy we were all there; she was grateful. We wanted to do everything we could for her and Denny and the boys; we just wanted to be near her. We were all as grateful to be there as she was to have us there.

The Christmas holiday was nearing, and Nena wanted the house decorated, the baking done, the gifts wrapped, and on and on and on. She had so much to do and was so worried she wouldn't have time to get it all done. I made her a deal, a deal she couldn't refuse. I suggested that she have a nice long afternoon nap after we finished lunch and that she would have a huge surprise when she got up. She laughed at the idea but agreed..

Nena ate very slowly these days, so we all paced ourselves to do the same. As we ate, we talked about wrapping the presents she bought for her boys; she tried hard to remember where she stashed all of them. We talked about where we would have our Christmas dinner and what we would eat.

Nena was finally ready for her nap, so the boys took her to her bedroom and lay her down, propping big fluffy pillows all around her. We turned off the lights, leaving only a small nightlight on that made beautiful shadows in the room. I told her, as I kissed her goodnight, that I'd be checking in on her often. She asked me to stay with her; my heart skipped a beat as I cuddled alongside her. She was crying quietly and asked me to just hold her. I let her cry while I assured her that everything would be okay.

I asked her if she could describe how she felt inside her body. She said her lungs felt tight, like they had been inflated. She had no strength to pick up her feet to walk, and the pressure in her head was worse than everything else, sometimes like her head would just explode. She never used the word "pain"; she always referred to it as pressure.

Just then, someone in the kitchen dropped something, and she twitched; I was holding her with my whole body wrapped around

a Sibling's Story

her, and I told her to just rest now and that everything was going to be all right. I held her very still and paced my breathing with hers. Her trembling turned into softness as she drifted into a short but restful nap.

When she woke up, she was grateful that I was still there, holding her. She remarked about her restful nap and lay still for another few minutes, just enjoying the quiet and comfort. She was ready to go into the front room to see what all the other siblings had decorated.

Before Nena took her nap, I took Markie into the basement and showed him where all her Christmas decorations were; that included a tree and a train set. I asked him to set up the train and the little village on her desk; they were free to do whatever they wanted to do after that. They did an outstanding job. Nena was so happy, she cried; we all cried. We all cried for different reasons, and we all cried for the same reasons. Nena was razzle-dazzled over her house; it had been decorated for the holidays while she napped.

The front room had windows halfway up the walls on three sides. It's a long narrow room with patio doors that lead into the rest of the house; it was an add-on to the original house. At first, she used this room as a greenhouse, starting all her seeds, vegetables, and flowers in late winter so the plants would be ready to set out in the garden by late spring. Another greenhouse was built a few years later, so this room was turned into a beautiful living room with a fantastic view in three directions. This was where her recliner, two full-size couches, entertainment center, and desk were.

Amy and Markie cleared that desk and created a little village with a small train running through it. Everything in the room was decorated from top to bottom. Small lights were strung around doorways and curtain rods, and all were covered with garland. Angels and snowmen and homemade ornaments were hanging or sitting everywhere; it was so festive.

The artificial tree was put together, and it sat by Nena's recliner. When the boys got home from school, they would help Nena decorate it. Nena sat in her chair, looking at all her pretty Christmas decorations while she waited for her sons to get off the bus. From her chair, she could see the bus turning the corner; she could see everything from her chair.

I watched and listened from the doorway as my brothers and sisters talked. I wondered what Nena was thinking, or even if she could. I wondered what the treatments had done to her thought process. She was still in total denial, even though the drugs were no longer able the control the seizures.

I looked at this beautiful room as an atmosphere for passing; it was a warm, happy, and peaceful setting. It overflowed with love.

The boys came home from school, all excited after seeing the room decorated, and eager to put the ornaments on the tree. Nena sat on the couch with her sons, unwrapping each precious ornament while telling its story. The unwrapping became very challenging, and the stories became blurred; another seizure, another scare. Together, we all got through it.

The little boys were getting used to witnessing the seizures and watching as their elders got their mom back in control. They got to stay at their stepsister's house that night, while Denny, my siblings, and I tended to Nena around the clock.

Hospice and Family

ALTHOUGH HER DISCOMFORT WAS increasing, Nena was still happy to visit with her friends. Her best friend from high school (and very close friend to this day) stopped by for a visit. Debbie joined us girls on more than one occasion at the hospital in Madison for doctor's appointments and for our lunches afterwards. Debbie was a nurse and had been very helpful, explaining many medical terms and procedures or protocol to us during and since Nena's original diagnosis. We gave Debbie some alone time with Nena while the rest of us did other things around the house.

Before Debbie left the following morning, she had a chance to speak privately with Amy; they, too, had been very good friends since they were little girls. She expressed to Amy that in her opinion, medically speaking, it was time to call hospice. She said her goodbyes to all of us and to her best friend since childhood and then left for home.

We all knew how Nena felt about hospice, but after talking it over with Denny and the siblings, we decided to make the call.

The first call I made was to Nena's doctor in Madison. I described to him our sister's condition and that we needed some things for her: stronger medicine and oxygen. The doctor agreed, so I made a call to an old friend of mine who worked closely with hospice. I explained to her about Nena's feelings toward hospice, but now the family had to request help.

We would need someone to bring everything to us, explain what to do and how, and then we would want her to leave. I explained that we, Nena's family, would be tending to her every need. This was the call that set everything in motion, and within hours the items that I asked for were being delivered.

While I was organizing our new plan over the phone, the others were explaining to Nena what was going to be happening: that it would only help her. The only thing that made it all right with Nena was that the nurse would only come and show us how to do what was needed and then she would leave. Nena was glad that we were going to stay with her; we were not leaving.

The pressure in her head and the anxiety attacks were becoming too much for Nena; it made her aware that hospice was the right thing to do. We needed this additional help to take better care of her.

Making the necessary calls and speaking to various doctors and nurses was a heartfelt experience for me. I was making plans to insure the quality of the last days of my sister's life. I was making plans for this family to lose yet another precious life. I was preparing myself. My mood became somber as I ordered each piece of equipment I thought we might need, knowing what each machine was used for and what each piece could or could not do. I knew that it wouldn't be long before my sister would meet in the garden with God. I also knew that Nena was still in denial.

Within a short period of time, people began to deliver the various medical equipment that we needed. The nurse from Hospice arrived and made her assessment; explaining to Nena the degree of her condition. She also explained about different drugs that could eliminate or reduce the pressure, pain, and anxiety she was feeling. She also expressed to Nena that she had never walked into any of her patients' homes and felt the kind of love that she felt when we walked into Nena's house. The nurse then told Nena that if she could do anything else for her, to feel free to call anytime, day or night. Nena was receptive and agreed.

a Sibling's Story

Denny, my siblings, John-John, and I gathered around the kitchen table, along with the nurse, to hear how to operate the different machines. We no longer had to give Nena any shots; it was now a morphine pump that was computer-programmed. There would be fewer pills, but we'd have to give her breathing treatments and bolis shots through the IV we had hooked up through the port that was inserted in her chest from previous medical procedures.

The schedule for the drugs and medications was originally set up for the least amount of dosage, but it became quickly evident that it was not enough. Additional calls were made, and the dosages were increased. We were then able to stay ahead of sister's pain and pressures and seizures and anxieties. We maintained a rigid schedule of the drugs, medications, and breathing treatments and documented everything in detail.

Each day, I would check in with and report to the local drugstore that was dispensing Nena's drugs. They constantly reassured me that we were doing everything right and respected any decision the family made regarding additional meds or anything else. They were all very impressed with this constant vigil by a family who so loved their youngest sibling, wife, and mother.

The calls I made to anyone in the medical field during these days were received very graciously in their recognition of a beautiful love, a love that can only be found within real family.

Everything seemed to be happening so quickly. I knew I'd have to talk to Denny soon about the things he wouldn't want to hear. I took my time thinking it through and getting things lined out in my own mind. I needed to be strong and have everything in the proper perspective.

People are not usually prepared for death and dying, not just the medical, physical, and mental parts, but the part that comes after the actual death. The details. Fortunately, over many years, I've had the opportunity to deal with these most important details. I've watched and I've learned well. I know how to make things easier, and I know who to share this knowledge with.

I chose my time and asked Denny if we could talk privately. I explained to him that I didn't mean to pry into his personal business, but I knew some things that could help him secure everything without getting the state involved in his business after my sister's passing.

I had been privy to some of Nena's personal business over the years, and I knew first-hand that she and Denny had some separate, individual bank accounts and some properties that were not titled properly for the process Denny was going to be facing shortly. I also asked him to consider talking to the funeral home director. I tried to make him understand the legalities and the urgency to get these things done. We discussed these personal issues, and Denny agreed, asking me to accompany him; I said yes. I was grateful.

After breakfast the following morning, Denny said he needed to pick up some groceries and had some errands to run and that he'd be back shortly. It was also his company's Christmas party, and he thought he should at least make an appearance. Nena told him that he should go and eat with his friends and co-workers. He didn't want to go without her, so she suggested that he take me in her place. I agreed.

After we left, everyone just went on as usual: getting Nena bathed and dressed and relaxed and anything else they could do while Denny and I started working on the long list I prepared.

We started with the banks; the wording needed to be changed on all their accounts, including the boys' accounts. The wording on the real estate they owned also needed to be changed; the words "and/or" may seem like very small words, but the impact they have in legal issues is very large. Denny didn't realize, until now, just how important this was; the bank officers agreed with everything he was doing.

After all the banking was done, we took a ride on the back roads, gazing at nature's wonders and gently discussing the remainder of things we had left to do. I shared with Denny a few stories concerning families who didn't own up to their responsibilities before a loved one passed. I made him understand how unpleasant it is for everyone when 911 has to be called upon a death, as opposed to a funeral director. I had witnesses both ways, and I wanted my sister's passing to be beautiful; I wanted the removal of her tired body to be without stress. It can be this way or it could get so out-of-hand so quickly.

People's emotions at the time of death can cloud all logical thought and decision-making. I thought it best to make these important decisions about arrangements while we were still somewhat clear in our thinking. Denny wanted these things too and was grateful to be made aware of and have help making everything right, at least as right as the circumstances would allow.

He wondered where the right place would be for her viewing and funeral. He drove me to a cemetery on one of those back country roads where several of his ancestors were buried. I knew when I saw it that Nena's body should be laid to rest there. It was remote, peaceful, and beautiful, in spite of winter's coat. Denny asked for and respected my input; it was very emotional and yet very businesslike. We made the decision that this cemetery was the best location.

We left the cemetery and headed into town to the funeral home; we decided it would be a halfway point for friends and family to gather for Nena's wake.

Since I knew the director personally, I introduced Denny and then explained the circumstances that brought us to him. It was important, for many reasons to me, that these arrangements for my sister be given our utmost clear-minded attention.

Mr. Larson and Denny spoke, although I don't know about what. I was sitting right there but couldn't hear a thing because my thoughts were running crazy. I knew that Mr. Larson would get up soon and lead us to the room that was filled with coffins.

As my thoughts were processing, he rose from his chair, and Denny and I followed him into this room. I held it all together, and when he left us alone after the tour, I was able to help Denny decide which one would be Nena's.

Nena loved anything with angels; her house, inside and out, supported the angel craze. And so, how fitting that we should have an angel on the inside lid of the casket we chose for her.

Because we had taken this step, it would make things a lot easier after Nena passed. After a person dies, as long as prior arrangements are made, the funeral director is the one who arrives with the coroner and pronounces the death. He then takes the body out of the home without involving the police, ambulance, or hospital. The business arrangements were finalized.

As we were leaving, Mr. Larson handed me some papers and asked me to fill them out when I had a chance. I knew they were life history and obituary forms that needed to be filled out in detail and ready for him at my sister's passing. I placed the papers in my purse, and then Denny and I left.

We already had a traumatic and emotional day, but we still needed to talk to the minister of their church. We wanted to let her know the circumstances, and we wanted to find out how the church would handle the service and the luncheon afterwards.

Nena was born and raised a little Catholic girl, but she married out of the church. From time to time, she and the boys attended the small Presbyterian Church near their home; Denny was not much of a religious man. I told my brother-in-law that Nena should have a church service; it's just the way it had to be. For Nena.

The preacher lady knew Nena and was happy to do anything she could for her and her family. We discussed the service at the church and the graveside service. I requested the Ladies Auxiliary to provide a luncheon afterwards in the church basement at the family's expense. Everything was agreed upon.

With one more detail checked off our list, we knew that we had to go back home and act as thought nothing happened, back to Nena and the family. We accomplished a lot, and yet we had to behave as if everything was good; and it really was.

a Sibling's Story

We all took advantage of the times that Nena was awake. Members of Denny's family made brief visits. They were told to speak only in low tones but to speak freely to her and say what they needed to say. Some realized how critical the situation was, and some didn't.

She visited with her mother- and father-in-law, the two people in her life that took over the responsibilities of her own parents over the last twenty years. I don't think they realized how rough the situation really was for Nena. They weren't alone. It's hard for anyone to accept that someone so young and so beautiful with so much life ahead of her can be here today and gone tomorrow. But that's just the way it happens.

Another night, she got to visit with her brother-in-law Jackie, and his beautiful wife, Sylvia. It had been only what seemed to be a short period of time since they last saw her; they left with very heavy hearts. It's hard for anyone to see the progression cancer has on a body. It was very hard on both Jackie and Sylvia.

Her favorite nieces, on Denny's side, also stopped by one evening. Unfortunately, Nena was asleep during this time, so I sat with them on the couch as they watched their beautiful aunt sleeping; it was very hard for the lovely, teenage girls. I knew how much my sister had taught them over the years and that, one day, their lives would be changed because of something Aunt Nena had either said to them or had done for them.

The most heart-wrenching visit with anyone from Denny's side of the family was with her grown stepchildren. They had been in and out of the house since we all arrived and took over. During their last brief visit, I spoke to each of them privately and told them that time was very short; if they had anything they wanted to get right with Nena or if there was anything they wanted or needed to say, they should do it. Time was of the essence, and they came.

I knew, when they got there that evening, that they would be saying their goodbyes and that it would be very emotional. I stayed with them as they spoke to Nena, for a couple of reasons; if the emotions caused Nena more stress, I'd be right there for her in case she needed any medications, and because I wanted to hear them tell her how much they loved her and wanted to see their faces when my sister told them how much she loved them, how much they had added to her life.

I was so proud of these two young adults because they said all the things my sister needed to hear. When Nena spoke to them and told them what they needed to hear, their faces looked upon the woman who had lovingly helped raise them, and they could feel her unconditional love for them. I felt honored to have witnesses this beautiful exchange of love between a stepmother and her stepchildren.

We, as the caregiver team, limited any other visits, as each day was becoming harder for Nena. We, as her family, enjoyed our time with her, not only as a family united, but also on an individual basis. The bond between siblings had grown immensely. John-John's presence in all of this was becoming more and more important.

We all ate together, usually without even cooking because Denny and Nena's neighbors and friends had been most generous and thoughtful during these days, bringing us casseroles and soups and delicious Christmas treats.

We slept together, either with the little boys or on the couches near Nena. Denny slept in a sleeping bag near the Christmas tree, and someone always sat on the stool next to her recliner.

As a family, we did all the household chores; we did homework, as well as the laundry. We laughed and we prayed and we tended to Nena. There were no inhibitions; she was bathed and cleaned and was always dressed in her fancy nightwear, resting in her recliner on fresh bedding.

When Nena wasn't sleeping, she would visit with us. We spoke of days long since passed, when we were kids. We talked about our parents, our married lives, and parenthood, all the good times and, of course, the bad times. We concluded that we all turned out to be extremely outstanding individuals; all our lives were different, but nonetheless, we were loving and caring people. This fact remained: when the chips were down, the sibling bond held strong.

I was very proud of my siblings, my brother-in-law, and my three young nephews. My siblings' spouses and all my nieces and nephews displayed outstanding loyalty during the days and nights they were alone without Scottie, Markie, and Amy. This would also include my husband, George, being without me.

There were also some difficult times in each household while we were away from home. Sometimes, all the times, tensions were running on the high-end for everyone. Each of us was dealing with it as best as we could. Each was different, and yet each was the same. In my estimation, my family rallied together; in whatever role we played and through our common bond, we were a family united.

My brother-in-law, David, and my sisters-in-law, Cat and Barbara, picked up the slack of their missing spouses. As hard as it was for each of them, they must have been so very proud. When they did get to speak to their spouses, either by phone or to see them only briefly once or twice, how brave they all were, for it must have broken their hearts to see and hear the pain that their loved one was going through.

They showed genuine commitment and consideration throughout Nena's battles. They all showed tremendous strength, running their households and businesses. They displayed the courage and love to help their children through this difficult period. They managed to keep themselves together because they all loved Nena; they all did what they had to do. All of them.

My nephew, Chase, twelve-years-old, had a very difficult and angry approach to dealing with this recent event of watching his mother grow weaker and sicker, watching his aunts and uncles taking care of her and comforting him and his little brother.

Everything that was happening all around him was totally out of context. He enjoyed the fact that we were all there together, but he didn't like it. I didn't blame him for that.

John-John played a big part in helping Chase. They could talk, both Chase and Cole Jesse. They had a link other than being only cousins to John-John. The little boys would soon be walking in their older cousin's moccasins. They could speak on another level apart from any of the rest of us.

Cole Jesse was the soft touch. At ten-years-old, he couldn't get enough of being with his mom. Sometimes he'd realize what was really happening, and I'm sure we could all agree that it was ultimately something John-John said to him that made him understand and accept. In a different way.

My sister Nena was well aware of what she was seeing. It may not have been in the seeing for her as much as it was the feeling of John-John's goodness and character and charisma. My nephew's presence within the family was, indeed, extremely important. No one could have done or said the things he did to the little boys like he did. It was the reason and the meaning for John-John's original dream; it was what he could do to help the family and be a part of this beautiful experience. I watched my nephew accept his place and role with honor within the family. All of his cousins looked up to him, and they all knew that if John-John said it, whatever it was, then it must be right.

Each day that passed, John-John helped do whatever he could as he doted on his Aunt Nena. I could see that as the days passed by, Nena was finally realizing how fine a young man John-John had grown up to be. Although John-John had lost his dad so many years ago, Nena realized that he had grown into this loving, caring, and self-confident man.

I know that he really helped her to, somehow, just know and feel that her sons would come out of this with the help of all the family. Through it all, they would be all right and grow up to be very good men.

Nena had shown her sons about love, life, and laughter. She instilled in them the values that would undoubtedly be the principals of how they would live their lives. She knew the families would watch over and take care of Denny and the boys.

There is no Death, Only a Change of Worlds

One sunny afternoon, the house was quiet, and the sun was shining brightly throughout the house. We watched the cardinals and blue jays feeding and flying about outside. The only sound we heard was the oxygen machine.

My brothers and my sister, Amy, each had to leave for a few hours to connect with their own families. Denny was outside tending to the necessary chores, and the little boys were at school. John-John and I were alone with Nena; she felt pretty good, and we were having a great visit.

My nephew was sitting on the couch directly in front of Nena, and I was perched on the stool beside her recliner. We weren't into a deep conversation, just pleasant chitchat; sister was telling John-John about the pheasants they watched out the same window from time to time. It was a normal, uneventful exchange of light conversation.

As Nena spoke, she went right from talking about the beautiful pheasants strutting through the yard to looking directly into John-John's eyes, speaking to him as if she was speaking more directly to his dad, our brother Johnnie.

She called him by name and had a beautiful conversation with Johnnie. She told him how sorry she was that he missed out on so much over the last thirteen years since he passed, how very good John-John turned out to be, but she was sure that he already knew that. She said she was sure that she knew that only he and she and Nanc knew certain things for which she was grateful: things like his ways of intervening at the most opportune times. Her eyes never left John-John's eyes during this vision.

Neither my nephew nor I moved or hardly even took a breath as she spoke. We both knew we were witnessing a very spiritual experience. When she finished expressing her feelings to my brother, she immediately went back to John-John and the conversation we were having before, talking now about the hummingbirds that gather near the window where she always hangs the red feeders and calling him by his name. We acted as though nothing had happened because it was obvious that sister had no recollection of what we had just witnessed.

For me, that beautiful event was my sign that Nena was being helped to accept death by my brother, who was working his magic through his son and me. It was also a sign for me that Nena really did believe in help from beyond and knew that some of the prior happenings during her illness were real, very real, even though she never really understood during the times of unusual occurrences.

I sought my brother's help many times when I couldn't be physically present with my sister. The first time Nena really experienced Johnnie's spiritual existence was when she was in the bone marrow unit. Amy and I had already been with her for several days but decided to go home for a day or so and that I'd return with my brother Markie.

We were home only a short time when Nena called. She said she missed us already. Being in isolation was very hard on her, so we talked at length, and I tried, with words, to comfort her. Although she did feel better, I needed to do something else.

After I hung up the phone, I felt an urgency to call on some very powerful, spiritual friends: people who believe, people who pray, people who love. I called upon these friends and different family members across the country to take the time, at a certain hour of that day, and pray for strength and peace for my sister. They were all keeping Nena in their daily prayers, anyway, but were all honored to be part of this very powerful meeting of prayer.

Late that afternoon, only moments after this special prayer had taken place all across the land, Nena called. Her voice was shaken, and yet she spoke calmly. She asked if I had just done some of my "Nanc stuff"; I asked her to explain to me why she would ask me that.

The nurse had set her in the recliner and given her a Popsicle to eat; she said she ate it and then immediately fell asleep. She thought she'd been dreaming about Johnnie, and although she felt like she didn't want to wake up, she knew someone was in the room with her and she needed to wake up. She thought she saw Johnnie, all glowing and white, standing next to her bed in full view from the recliner. She was so scared that she quickly closed her eyes and sat there trembling in fear of what it all meant.

I told her that what happened was a good thing. It was Johnnie, and he was just letting her know that he is always nearby and that she's never alone. I told her how lucky she was to have had such a beautiful experience and if she was ever given another opportunity like this one, to keep her eyes open.

She was calmed by these words and then felt grateful for the experience. She was insistent upon thanking me because she was sure I had something to do with it all. I simply said that prayer is a very powerful tool.

Another incident occurred the day she had part of one lung and one rib removed. Denny, my siblings, and I were with Nena in the little room as she was being prepped for surgery. We were all nervous and worried on the inside, but we were all putting on a show for Nena. The surgical cart came to get her, and before she left the room, we all hugged and kissed her and said we'd be waiting for her to get back.

I walked alongside the cart as they wheeled her to the surgery doors; I bent over and whispered in her ear that Denny and her siblings would be waiting for her and that I made arrangements for Johnnie to be in surgery with her, holding her hand. I reassured her that she would come through the surgery. She did.

Several hours after she left recovery and was in her room, she told me that Johnnie was there, holding her hand during surgery. She could remember that her hand was warm, like it was being held. She knew he was there, even though she couldn't see him. The feeling she had inside of her made her realize that he was really there helping her get through this surgery.

I always took these times as a sign that talking to Johnnie and asking for his help with Nena was a powerful connection. Our loved ones who have passed are never far away from us. They are there, and when specifically called upon for help, they are ever near. I strongly believe there is no death, only a change of worlds. I believe too that there are angels that walk amongst us. I've had much proof in those beliefs over the years, and I am most grateful to have the knowledge to recognize the signs and determine the meanings and lessons to be learned. Sometimes.

Denny showed unlimited bravery during these last days. He had to keep up his strength to maintain and to realize these were, in fact, the last days. He graciously accepted all of us into his home to help in the care giving. He felt a family connection like he'd never known before. The power of love that filled his home was at times very overwhelming for him.

I was the person that Denny talked to; I mean really talked to. We had a common bond that united us, the fact that each of us was the spouse of a dying partner. No one can ever connect with you if they haven't walked in your moccasins. I respected him so much for allowing us in, making Nena's passing a beautiful part to the end of her life.

He showed bravery with his children, all four of them. He kept it together for the sake of his children and would let us help when we could. He was not selfish with anything. He was grateful for everything and everyone, all the while his heart breaking and his life forever changing with no direction. I listened to him and cried with him many times before, but this time, these last days, the realization of not having Nena anymore was a very heartfelt and emotional time for both of us.

He knew that his wife would leave this world soon and that he would be left to pick up all the pieces and carry on the best that he could, without her. He was realizing more and more each day just how much she had done for him and their kids, the work she had done and the sacrifices she had made in their lives together. Love had taken on a whole new meaning for my brother-in-law.

My brother Scottie was very much the big brother for Nena. His rough exterior and commanding voice could never override his mountainous capacity of love and compassion. Whatever he said to her, she believed. He was soft and tender with her and felt honored to be with her. I know how he made her feel when he wrapped his long, muscular arms around her; I'm sure she felt love and strength and power from him. He was the big, strong brother, and she was his baby sister; he had a powerful magic over her.

My brother Markie was altogether different. He was the little brother, her playful brother. During her last days, Markie made a game out of her foot rubs and her leg massages. He was the one who teased her and made her laugh. He was the one who cooked all of us special meals in Nena's kitchen. Markie played a big role in keeping proper records and reading or adjusting the medical equipment.

The differences they might have had were forever forgiven. He treated her so lovingly; he bestowed all his pleasant nature on her. Markie, as well as brother Scottie, was honored to carry her from room to room and to be an intricate part of her health care.

Amy was also a big part of the recordkeeping and medical equipment procedures. Amy and Markie handled it very well;

they were a remarkable team. I praise them for their strategic and well-educated minds.

Amy's love for Nena was unquestionable. They had their differences in the past, but in the last few years, they rebuilt a beautiful sisterhood. During these last days, Amy showed tremendous love and genuinely displayed her love in many ways.

Amy did everything she could for Nena and was also an important figure with Chase and Cole Jesse. Amy was a mom also, and she was the one to make sure the boys got their homework done, brushed their teeth, and took their baths. She read to Cole Jesse, and he read to her. The time Amy spent with the boys during this time made Nena very happy.

Amy was also the mastermind behind the beautiful Christmas room that was decorated in Nena's honor. Nena was very grateful for this room that held so much family love and unity.

And then of course, everyone's favorite, George. Nena and George had many things in common; the biggest factor now was cancer. They were very good friends, as well as in-laws, and had many private talks over the years. I know he always helped her, but in the last few years, they grew closer and closer.

I believe that George was very instrumental in helping Nena accept and forgive all the negative things in her life. He had a way with words, and when he said anything, you just knew you could believe it. He was always an important part of Chase and Cole Jesse's lives, and she loved him for that. After all, he was the one who taught the boys how to play poker.

George was adamant about his schedule for cancer, letting nature take its course, and Nena was just as adamant about hers. They understood each other and each other's ways. For George, watching her go through all those treatments and watching her body be ravaged was very stressful and taxing, not only on his physical health but even more on his heart—his soulful heart.

I watched as George's health grew worse, and I watched as Nena's health grew worse. I was torn many times as to where to be. How I would inevitably decide was to anticipate who was the sickest out of the two. I would be with one and feel guilty for not being with the other. I wanted everything to be perfect for both of them at all times. Even though George was having a difficult physical and emotional time, Nena was sicker, and I was needed with her.

He was very understanding about my loyalty toward my sister. He knew I was where I needed to be during these last days, not only for sister but also for the entire family. He had to do whatever it took to take care of our household as my brothers' wives and sister's husband had to do in their absence.

Each family member had his or her specialty. My job was to organize and delegate, in other words, be the boss. I maintained this position within the family because of my seniority; being the oldest sibling, I've been the boss since they were all born.

My love for my baby sister was always intense. Nena seemed to be the one who needed my coveting nature. These last years, since her diagnosis, I was the one with her most of the time. We shared much and we spoke openly. I listened to her scream and saw her angry, held her when she cried, and listened when she needed to talk, as well as talked when she needed to listen. I always tried to have the right and good words to say.

Our sisterhood was extreme. There were no secrets; she let me into her true self. She had become a woman of strength in her own right.

Saturday morning, Nena took a turn for the worse. She wasn't really communicating. She slept a lot, and her breathing was becoming more labored. We tried to implement extra breathing treatments, but nothing seemed to help. We were able to keep her comfortable and calm; someone always had a hand placed on her at all times so that she could feel a loving touch. It was obvious that major organs were shutting down.

Nightfall came, and Chase got to stay overnight with his stepsister. Scottie and Amy each had company Christmas parties to go to, so they left to attend them even though they didn't want to leave Nena. It had started snowing, and from inside the beautifully decorated room, I sensed a peacefulness I hadn't felt before. I felt that this night would be very special.

Sister was letting go; we made her as comfortable as possible.

Cole Jesse kissed his mom goodnight, and Uncle Mark took him to bed. He told him not to be kicking him when he went to bed, and Cole Jesse just laughed. He was happy that Uncle Mark was going to sleep with him.

Several hours passed by, and Nena seemed to be calmer. Markie, Denny, and John-John all laid down for a while; Markie was with Cole Jesse in the bedroom, John-John on the couch in the next room, and Denny was on the couch near Nena.

I sat on the couch directly in front of her, praying. After Denny fell asleep, I prayed to her and for her, out loud. I knew she could hear me even though I spoke just barely over a whisper. I could see her try to open her eyes, but only a tear would fall. I was at her side touching her and rocking her. I quietly told her that everything would be all right.

Markie came in to check up on us. He wanted to do another breathing treatment, and I told him that it was no longer necessary; that it would do no good. He agreed and went into the kitchen.

I told her that the boys were snuggled safe and warm in bed and that Denny was sleeping on the couch next to her. I told her how proud I was of her and how much I loved her. She was such a good mom and wife and the best sister ever. I told her the boys would be good because their daddy would see to it. I assured her that Denny would be fine and that he would not disappoint her.

She heard me; I felt her. I told her that it was okay to go and that she should reach up and take Johnnie by the hand because he had a special place he wanted to take her; it was time to go home. Her arm lifted slightly as though she was wanting to reach for her brother's hand.

Within seconds, she drew her last breath; she was peaceful. I sat there for a moment, maybe longer, feeling a spiritual presence, like a glow. I felt that my brother and sister were running and playing together somewhere in a most splendid world with no pain or problems. The pain and torture of not being herself for so long was gone. Sister was now free to roam and watch from afar. I felt her freedom and rejoiced silently for her in her newfound home.

I stood and walked toward my brother in the kitchen. Softly, I said, "Please check sister for a pulse." He put his arm around me and together we went back into the beautiful Christmas room.

Markie shut off the machines and took all the equipment off of and out of her body. I cleaned her and straightened her clothes and blankets. Markie knelt down beside the couch and woke Denny to tell him of his wife's passing. We remained quiet. I was aware of everything around me; I soaked up the goodness and contentedness of the energy in the room. It was tranquil. Sister was still, no frowns from pain or anger.

I went in to wake John-John, and we all consoled each other. We then decided what needed to be done next.

The silence in the house, without the oxygen machine running and the morphine pump pumping, was unnerving to me. I phoned Scottie and Amy, then George. I told George I'd be home, but not right away; I needed to help Denny with the rest of the arrangements. Denny made the rest of the calls to family and friends while I got Nena's outfit together for her wake.

It wasn't daylight yet, and it had been snowing all night: eight inches of fresh fallen snow.

Someone was always looking out for Cole Jesse to wake up. We had moved him into his mom's bedroom, near the back of the house, after she had passed. We didn't want them to take the body past Cole Jesse's bedroom in case he woke up.

Scottie and Amy arrived shortly after they were notified, before 5:30 a.m., each driving through the unplowed roads.

We all gathered around her and said our silent prayers. We were all so quiet and yet happy for Nena that she didn't hurt anymore. The reality of it all was felt differently by each of us.

There was much to be done now. The coroner and funeral director had driven through the snow-covered back roads. I had already gathered the things they'd need to present my sister for her final viewing.

The papers Mr. Larson gave us, when we previously contacted him, was a History of Life form. We had all looked it over during the quiet moments in these last days and wrote down dates and memorable events: what she liked and what she loved. We wrote who should bear her casket. Together, as a family, we managed to have it filled out for the funeral director.

We prepared ourselves for the things to come.

The final arrangements were made, and they took the body away. We all talked for a while, and soon everyone left; everyone had their own arrangements to make.

John-John and I stayed with Denny. I thought John-John should be nearby when Denny told Cole Jesse and Chase. He agreed to stay.

We were sitting in the front room, Denny in the blue overstuffed chair near the phone, John-John and I at the table. No one was really speaking, only thinking and waiting for Cole Jesse to wake up and for Chase to come home from his stepsister's house.

Cole Jesse came staggering out of his mom's bedroom, knowing he didn't fall asleep there. He was rubbing his big brown eyes when his dad asked him to come to him. Cole Jesse crawled up in his dad's lap and snuggled under his arm.

With tears in his eyes, Denny told him that the angels had come and had taken Mom to heaven. Cole Jesse looked up at his dad and said, "She's gone?" Denny nodded yes. Cole Jesse climbed off his dad's lap and went into the bathroom and closed the door behind him without another word or tear.

We just sat there, all of us so taken with the moment. We sat there motionless. We let some time pass, and then Denny finally knocked on the door and went in. Cole Jesse was wiping the tears from his eyes, acting like such a big boy. Denny carried him out, and they sat down together in the chair where I'm sure they sat many times before to have their talks.

A car pulled into the driveway; it was Chase. I took Cole Jesse and John-John into the beautiful Christmas room; the room where he last saw his mom resting in the recliner. The recliner was empty. The three of us sat on the couch and just held each other while Denny told Chase about mom. While we held and comforted Cole Jesse, Denny and his daughter did the same with Chase.

I was proud of the boys. The thoughts that must have been going on in their minds was hard for me to even comprehend. I could not even imagine their pain. John-John took both of the little boys and sat with them on the steps leading down to the basement; what they said, only they know.

The phone started ringing; the neighbors began plowing and bringing food and flowers. Denny, his parents, and sister and I left to pick out the grave plot. Denny and I had chosen the cemetery; now he needed to buy the plot. Afterward, Denny and I stopped by the houses of the men we had chosen to be the pallbearers.

We had a pleasant ride together; the back roads looked like a winter wonderland. It was a beautiful day in early December. A flock of Cardinals flew in front of us as we drove and, a little farther down the road, a flock of Blue Jays. It was rare to see flocks of these songbirds, but it seemed fitting that we should experience this beauty on such a blessed day.

We passed the property that Denny and Nena had bought several years before. She loved walking the hundred and eighty acres. She had a family picture taken in her favorite spot of Denny, Nena, her stepchildren, and her sons. She loved that picture. Nena would never walk on the hills and bluffs, now covered in a deep blanket of snow, again.

After we spoke to the pallbearers, who were honored to be asked, we continued on to finalize the funeral home and church arrangements. When we got back to Denny's, I said my goodbyes and headed home.

I was away for many days. The roads were slippery, so it seemed to take forever to get home. George was waiting for me to arrive. I had called him shortly after Nena passed, and that was ten hours earlier. He made a bowl of his famous Mrs. Grass Chicken Soup with an Egg; we ate together and we talked and we cried.

Every time I looked at George, I was silently grieving my next loss. George took Nena's passing hard; it hurt him deep down inside. His breathing was worse, and I knew it the minute I saw him. My absence, Nena's death, and his own cancer-ridden body had taken a big toll on him. I could see it; I could sense it and I knew it.

My beautiful sister, forty years old, was buried in a lovely country cemetery near her home on December 12, 2000.

Epilogue

You have just read the beautiful story about Nena, and my hope is that you were also touched by her. In anticipation of your vested interest in George, I have begun to write you his story, which will be published at a later date.

God Bless You,
Nancy Seriani

Author Bio

NANCY SERIANI WAS BORN the eldest of six in a southwestern Wisconsin farming community in the early 1950s. From an early age, she took on the responsibility of caring and nurturing. In the years that followed, when family members fell ill, Nancy cared for and nurtured them without hesitation. Now, in addition to dealing with health issues of her own, Nancy continues to love, care for, and nurture others in need.

www.ingramcontent.com/pod-product-compliance
Lightning Source LLC
LaVergne TN
LVHW012117070526
838202LV00056B/5751